In this glossary:

[a] is pronounced as in f<u>a</u>r
[e] is pronounced as in g<u>e</u>t
[ee] is pronounced as in f<u>ee</u>t
[i] is pronounced as in s<u>i</u>t
[o] is pronounced as between g<u>o</u>t and g<u>oa</u>t
[oo] is pronounced as in l<u>oo</u>se
[y] is pronounced as in <u>y</u>es

[zh] is pronounced as in vi<u>si</u>on

The Raspberry Hut

and Other Ukrainian Folk Tales
Retold in English

Edited by Danny Evanishen
Translations by John W Evanishen
Illustrations by Deanna Evanishen
and Johanne (Evanishen) Kasha

Published by
Ethnic Enterprises
Publishing Division
Summerland, BC
1994

Canadian Cataloguing in Publication Data

Main entry under title:

The raspberry hut

ISBN 0-9697748-2-6

1. Tales--Ukraine. I. Evanishen, Danny, 1945-
GR203.18.R37 1994   398.2'0947'71   C94-910220-2

Ethnic Enterprises
Publishing Division
Box 1324
Summerland, BC
V0H 1Z0

Printed and Bound in Canada
by New Horizon Printers
Summerland, BC

Table of Contents

Dedicated to my father, John W Evanishen, who started this folk tale project.

Foreword

This collection of Ukrainian folk tales began when my father, John W Evanishen, translated some stories he found in an old Ukrainian book his father had given him. The book was made up of parts of several books glued together and tattered with age and use. It was difficult to determine the titles of the books that had been put together or even their age. What was evident, however, was that here were some little-known tales which had come to us by sheer chance. It could be that there are no more copies of these little books in existence.

My father translated the tales for the enjoyment of his grandchildren, hoping to print a few copies to give them for Christmas. When he showed them to me, I was impressed with their quality and I began to investigate the subject. I found that nobody had ever undertaken to collect all the Ukrainian folk tales in Canada.

Through my research I discovered that there are thousands of Ukrainian folk tales, of which this volume comprises only a very small part. Further volumes are planned which will eventually see in print all the Ukrainian folk tales I am able to collect.

If anyone has any more tales they would like to contribute to future volumes, they could be sent to me c/o Ethnic Enterprises.

—Danny Evanishen, Editor

Acknowledgments

This book is the result of a lot of work by quite a number of people.

John W Evanishen, my father, got the whole project started, did all the translations, and provided a lot of guidance along the road.

Natalka Evanishen, my mother, provided one story and a lot of encouragement.

Deanna Evanishen, my niece, and Johanne (Evanishen) Kasha, my sister, did the art work.

Many of the hundreds of books used in my research were tracked down and brought in for my use by the staff at Okanagan Regional Library in Summerland and Kelowna, BC. Thanks to Deb Dolman, Irene Meheriuk, Imelda Kedge, Marie Hogue and Jan Carlson.

Some excellent material came from the library at the Ukrainian Orthodox Cathedral in Vancouver, through the help of Nancy Worobetz.

Encouragement and advice were plentifully supplied by Mrs Olga Vesey of North Vancouver who, along with Mrs V Symchych, produced one of the best books of Ukrainian folk tales in English that I have seen.

Thank you also to Dorene Fehr, who did much reading and advising on the project, and also took the photograph on the back cover.

— Danny Evanishen, Editor

The Bear From
That Other World

There was once a very rich landowner who had three sons. The older two liked sports and hunting and much excitement. Their favorite pastime was hunting deer. They loved hunting on horseback, often chasing their prey until the poor deer would drop from exhaustion. They also lost many horses by riding them to death.

The youngest son, whose name was Ivas, was quiet and kindly. He did not enjoy hunting, but used to feed the animals, such as birds, stray dogs and other creatures. He was kind to the people his father ruled and often shared a piece of bread with the poor. Instead of going out and chasing all over the country, he liked to stay at home. His two older brothers thought of him as an idler and somewhat of a little simpleton.

One day while his brothers were hunting, Ivas went for a walk in a nearby forest. As he walked, he could hear the baying of the hounds and the pounding hooves of galloping horses. The chase was on! Before long he saw a fawn running straight for him, being chased by his brothers. The weary animal fell at his feet and Ivas sat beside her, gently stroking her head. He begged his brothers not to kill the fawn, but to sell her to him. After teasing him about being so soft-hearted, they agreed and away they rode, laughing and yelling.

The delighted boy spent the rest of the day feeding and petting the fawn and then led her deep into the forest where she would be safe. The deer turned to him and said: "Thank you for saving my life. You have shown yourself to be a very kind person. Some day we will meet again and you will be glad that you saved my life." Then she disappeared into the forest. Ivas was astounded to hear the deer speak and stood stupefied for a long time before going home.

When he told his father and brothers what had happened they, of course, did not believe him and said that he was nothing but a fool.

Not long after this, the two older boys decided to go travelling and see the world. Their father gave them not only his permission but also plenty of money. He told them: "Go, my sons, as you see I am not stingy with money. However, there is one thing I would like you to do. See that you learn something useful while you are away. It would be a shame to spend that much money on pleasure alone. Go now, and I will await your return after one year has passed."

Both solemnly promised to return with something of worth and set off. In that one year they visited many strange countries, many beautiful cities and many magnificent castles.

In one village they came upon an orchard which interested them very much. It had many varieties of fruit trees which produced large and tasty fruit. They approached the owner and asked him to teach them about his orchard. They wanted to learn everything he knew. He agreed to teach them on the condition that they work with him for one year. This they were happy to do and, in that year, they learned much about the operation of a successful orchard.

Proud to have learned something useful, they returned home and proceeded to establish an orchard of their own. Ordering the best of everything from the orchard where they took their training, they grafted the new cuttings onto wild stock from their own area.

Ivas was very excited about the orchard and begged his father and brothers for permission to graft a tree for himself. "You little simpleton!" they said. "What do you know about grafting? Well, it will do no harm; you may as well go ahead and try it." His brothers gave him the poorest tree they had and he learned what to do by watching them in their orchard.

All excited, Ivas ran into the forest to the spot where he had met the fawn. Here there was a small wild pear tree. Not wishing to dig it up, he cut off a small branch which he took home and grafted onto his poor little tree.

Seeing his efforts, his two brothers roared with laughter. He had done it all backwards! But a strange thing happened. The grafting of the brothers failed, while that of Ivas succeeded. His poor little plant grew into a huge beautiful tree and, after some time, produced much beautiful fruit. Everybody was very impressed with the large golden pears.

After a while, Ivas noticed that each night a pear would disappear. The two older brothers set up a watch around the tree, but were unable to discover how another pear still went missing every night. Ivas asked his father to allow him to guard the pears one night. "How do you think you will do better than your smarter brothers who have failed to catch the thief?" asked his father but, at last, he agreed to let Ivas try.

Ivas had a high platform built by the tree and, that night, he sat upon it watching and waiting. Soon he began to doze off, but sat bolt-upright when he saw a lovely bird with golden feathers sit on the tree and pluck a pear. He grabbed for the bird but got only a tail feather, and the bird flew off with the pear. In the morning, Ivas told his father what had happened, and showed him the feather.

"Now we know who is stealing our pears," said the father. "If only we could somehow find and capture that bird."

"Let me go and search for it," said the eldest brother. The father agreed, giving him plenty of money and the finest horse. "If I do not return in one year or send word to you, that will mean that I am in trouble and you should send my brother to look for me," said the son.

The father waited for a year, but there was no sign of his son. What had happened was he had stopped overnight at an inn which was run by a group of gangsters. There he had become involved in gambling and lost not only all his money but even his horse. Since he had been unable to pay what he owed the crooks, they had stripped him of his belongings and thrown him into a dungeon, planning to kill him later.

When the year was up, the second son set out to find his brother. He came to the same inn, was also lured into gambling, lost everything like his brother had done and wound up in the dungeon with his brother.

After another year passed and there was no sign of the brothers, Ivas asked his father for permission to go and search for them and the golden bird. "You had better stay at home," said the father. "Your brothers were much smarter than you and they disappeared. One never knows what could happen to you."

Ivas begged so hard that finally the father relented and let him go. Not willing to risk much with Ivas, he gave him a small amount of money and an old nag to ride.

Ivas set out on his journey. Because he had little money, he did not stop at the inn. He travelled for many days until he came to a large river. While looking for a crossing he saw the body of a drowned man lying on the bank. He thought to himself, "It is not right for a body to lie there like that. Wild animals or vultures will tear it to pieces. It could happen to me some day." He rode to a nearby village and entered a small church where he told the priest about the dead man. He left money for the burial expenses, even selling his old horse to cover the costs.

Continuing his journey on foot, he kept up his search for his brothers and for the golden bird. Following a road that led through a large forest, he came face to face with a huge bear and was so frightened that he could not move. To his amazement, the bear spoke to him. "My name is Medvid," said the bear. "Where are you going, and why are you so sad?"

Ivas was very surprised to hear the bear talk, not realizing that this bear was the spirit of the drowned man he had buried. Ivas overcame his fear and surprise and told the bear about the search for his brothers and the golden bird.

"I know where this bird is," said Medvid. "It is far from here, in the palace of the goddess Jevlena, who takes care of all living creatures. Jevlena has two sisters: Naya, the goddess of kindness and Lada, the goddess of beauty.

"Not everyone can enter their palaces; one must be a kindly and honest person to do that. I will take you to the palace of Jevlena and the golden bird. But remember, when you find the room where the bird is kept, do not take the cage but only the bird; otherwise, it will go badly for you. Now climb on my back and hold tight."

Ivas sat on the bear, who bounded into the air and flew to the palace. It was set in a beautiful park surrounded by a stone wall with many turrets spaced many lengths apart.

Following the directions of the bear, Ivas entered the palace and found the room where the bird was kept in a golden cage, which was all decorated with precious stones. Seeing the splendid jewels, Ivas completely forgot the warning and reached out for the cage.

Suddenly there was a loud clanging, then a clap of thunder and a flash of bright light in which he saw a beautiful woman, like an angel, who said to him: "You were greedy! It was not enough for you to take the bird, but you also wanted to take the cage. For this you do not deserve to live; however, because of your kindness to others and for saving the life of a certain fawn, I will forgive you. I will give you the bird and the cage, but first you must bring me the horse with the golden mane from the palace of my sister Naya."

There was another clap of thunder and she disappeared. Ivas found himself outside the gate where Medvid was waiting for him.

Ivas told Medvid what had happened and that he must now fetch the horse with the golden mane. "I warned you not to touch the cage," said the bear, "but you did not heed my warning. You are lucky to be alive.

"I know where Naya lives," Medvid continued. "I will take you there. But remember, do not take the bridle. Take only the horse, or again you will be caught and things will go badly for you." Ivas promised to heed the warning.

He was taken to the palace of Naya, where he entered the grounds and made his way to the stable. There stood a beautiful horse, and beside the horse hung a splendid bridle. He thought to himself, "How can I ride a horse with no bridle?" and reached for it. There was a clap of thunder and Naya appeared in a flash of lightning.

"You have broken my rules and for this you should die. But, because you were kind to the creatures of the Lord, I will forgive you. I will give you the horse and the bridle, too. Now go to my sister Lada, who will give you her golden-haired daughter, Laryssa." With another clap of thunder, she disappeared.

Medvid was waiting for him outside the gate. "You disobeyed my instructions again, but once more were lucky. If you do not learn to do what you are told, some day you really will meet with great misfortune. Now I will take you to the palace of Lada. Her daughter knows you and will go with you. But for once, listen to what I tell you, as you may not be so lucky another time. Take Laryssa by the hand, but not the hand in which she will be holding a handkerchief. This is important, so do not forget."

Lada lived in another beautiful palace. Ivas followed the directions of the bear and found the room of Laryssa, the golden-haired maiden. She greeted him warmly and told him that she often took the form of a deer. She was, in fact, the fawn that he had saved from his two brothers.

Overcome by this fact and by her beauty, Ivas took her by the hand in which she held her handkerchief. No sooner had he done so than a clap of thunder rolled forth and, in a flash of lightning, Lada appeared before them. Ivas was so frightened that he dared not look at her.

"I know you and I know why you are here. As you are a kind and honest man, I will give you this maiden for your bride. But remember to conduct yourself in life according to the advice of wise and experienced people and all will be well with you. I will order a coach for you to take this maiden home for your wedding and will give you her dowry of gold and jewelry. Farewell and good luck to both of you." Having said that, Lada disappeared in another bright flash of lightning.

The golden coach was waiting for them outside the gate. Medvid was also waiting and once more chided Ivas for failing to follow instructions, but told him that he was again very lucky. They all went to the palace of Naya where they picked up the horse, which they took to the palace of Jevlena. There they left the horse and picked up the golden bird and the cage.

As they were preparing to return home, Medvid bade them farewell. Before leaving, he counselled Ivas further, saying that he was not always going to be so lucky and he really should follow the advice he is given. The bear also warned him: "Do not ransom anyone from prison who has been sentenced to death, no matter who that person is. Otherwise, things will go badly for you." He wished Ivas and Laryssa good health, sprang into the air and disappeared.

On the way home, they stopped at the inn where the two brothers were imprisoned. The gangsters were about to hang the two because they could not pay their debts. Recognizing his brothers, Ivas forgot the warning of the bear and bought their freedom from the evil men.

The brothers accompanied Ivas and Laryssa home. As they rode, they grew very envious of Ivas and his good luck. They were ashamed of their own failure and were afraid to come home empty-handed, so they plotted to kill him and take his riches for themselves.

As they came to a forest, the two brothers pretended to be thirsty and persuaded Ivas to help them find some water. Once out of sight of the coach, they fell upon Ivas and beat him badly. They threw him into a hollow, covered him with branches and left him for dead.

Returning to the coach, they told Laryssa that Ivas was killed by wolves and that they had barely escaped themselves. She was so shocked by this that she lost interest in everything. From then on, she spoke but little and became melancholy, brooding over Ivas and his ill-fortune. The two brothers tried to speak to her but failed to get any response.

When they got home, their father was very happy to see them and hugged his sons, as he had grieved for them so long. They lied to him about the fate of their brother and hid their own guilt. Introducing Laryssa to him and showing him the dowry and the golden bird, they had to admit that it was Ivas who had obtained all these riches. Because of the presence of Laryssa, they felt they had to tell the truth about this.

In the meantime, Medvid was feeling uneasy. Fearing that something terrible had happened to Ivas, he went to look for him. He soon found him in the hollow, covered with branches and near death. Steeping some herbs in hot water, Medvid forced the brew down the throat of the dying youth. After a time Ivas began to show signs of life and opened his eyes.

"I must have fallen asleep," he said. "Where is Laryssa and where are my brothers?"

"Certainly, you fell asleep!" said the bear. "You would have slept until judgment-day if it were not for me! Again you did not follow my advice, but ransomed your brothers. For this you nearly paid with your life." He then told Ivas what his brothers had done to him and that the maiden had gone home with them.

Medvid led Ivas to an old campfire where he took handfuls of ashes with which he told Ivas to cover his face and neck. He also made him rub his hands and arms in the ashes and Ivas came out looking like a dirty tramp.

"Now listen carefully to what I have to tell you," said Medvid, "and for your own sake, do exactly as I tell you. Go to the home of your father. Do not worry; no one will recognize you in this condition, as they all think that you are dead. Go to the head cook in the household and ask to be hired as a kitchen helper. Tell him you are covered with ashes as a penance and he will not question your appearance. When the time is right for you to reveal yourself, a sign will be given to you. If you heed my advice, good fortune will smile upon you. This is the last time I will be able to help you, as my stay on this earth has come to an end." Having said all this, Medvid vanished.

Ivas went home, resolving to faithfully follow the instructions of the bear. He thought about all his adventures and realized that he was wrong to disregard the good advice he had been previously given. This time, he would learn his lesson and do things the right way. As Medvid had promised, no one recognized him and he was hired by the cook, who made no inquiries.

The father and the two brothers did their best to console the sorrowful maiden. To try to cheer her, they arranged for a ball to which many guests were invited. It was on this occasion that the eldest brother was going to announce his betrothal to Laryssa.

On the night before the ball, Ivas had a dream in which Lada appeared to him. She brought him fine clothes to wear and gave him instructions to wash himself, dress up in the clothes and enter the ballroom at a certain time when all the guests would have arrived.

Awakening in the morning, Ivas found the clothes beside him. By this he knew that Lada still had him under her care and that this was the sign he was waiting for.

That evening, Ivas cleaned himself up and dressed in the fine clothes. When the right moment arrived, he walked into the ballroom. There was a silence and everyone wondered who the fine, handsome youth was who had just entered. No one had any idea until Laryssa cried out, "Ivas, my dearest!" and ran joyously to him.

The father then recognized his youngest son and, finally, the whole story was known. Everybody wanted to hang the two older brothers but, instead, the guards were called. They carried the two brothers to the court of the prince, who sentenced them to death.

Ivas appeared before the prince and begged him not to execute his two brothers. The prince reluctantly agreed to this, but still banished them from the country.

Ivas and Laryssa were soon married. They bought an old castle along with its forests and villages, and became wealthy and revered citizens of their country. Being kind-hearted, they earned the love and respect of their people.

The Clever Daughter

One day, a poor peasant found a brass mortar in the woods. "This bowl must have been used for making medicines," he thought, but he had no use for such a thing.

"I will take it to the boyar and sell it to him," he told his daughter when he came home.

"Do not bother," she said. "He will think it is worthless because it has no pestle to grind with. Boyars are often lacking in brains."

"But they do not lack money," her father answered. "It is worth a try."

When the boyar heard the offer, he took the bowl from the peasant and threw it out of the window. "What value is this with no pestle?"

"My daughter said you might not be very smart," muttered the peasant to himself as he headed for the door.

The boyar heard him and was very angry. "How dare she speak so of me? Very well. If she is so smart, tell her she must answer these three riddles or you will both be whipped soundly. First, what is the sweetest? Next, what is the richest? And finally, what is the sharpest? Come tomorrow with the correct answers."

The poor peasant went home wishing that he had never found the mortar, or that he had listened to his daughter. When he got home, he told his daughter what had happened.

"Do not worry," she said. "You will go to him tomorrow and answer his silly riddles."

"But I do not know the answers he wants," wailed the poor peasant.

"Father, here are answers he cannot quarrel with: the sweetest is sleep for, no matter what problems you have on this earth, when you sleep you leave everything behind; the richest is the Earth, because she feeds all of us; and the sharpest is the eye that can see through evil."

The father reluctantly went to the boyar the next day and gave him the answers. To his surprise, the boyar actually smiled when he heard them. "Your daughter must be a clever person indeed, for those are the very answers I was seeking. Let us now see just how clever she really is. Here are twelve eggs. Take them to your daughter and tell her to place a hen on them; by tomorrow, they must all be chicks."

"Well, how did it go with the boyar?" she asked her father when he got home.

"Oh, leave me in peace. The answers were correct, but now we are in more trouble than ever. He gave these twelve eggs to be hatched into chicks by tomorrow morning."

She looked carefully at the twelve eggs and laughed out loud. "A smart boyar he is, too!" she cried. "He even cooked these eggs for us!" She sat down and peeled all the eggs and she and her father made themselves a little feast right there.

"But what will I tell the boyar tomorrow?" he suddenly asked her.

"Take this handful of millet to him tomorrow. Tell him to thresh it, sow it, harvest it and flay it, for tomorrow I will have to feed it to the hungry chicks."

"Very well, I will do so. But who knows where this will all end?"

"Where are the chicks?" asked the boyar next morning, looking stern.

"My daughter has given me this millet for you. She says you must thresh it for her and sow it and harvest it and flay it, for she must feed it to the chicks today."

"Oh ho! So that is how wise she is! I must meet this clever daughter of yours. Tell her to come to me tomorrow, but listen carefully! She must come neither dressed nor naked, neither riding nor walking, and she must neither give me a gift nor not give me a gift."

Once more the poor peasant went home all worried. "Daughter, how can this be? We have begun with this boyar and now we will be lucky to come out of it with our skins."

He told her what the boyar had said, and she said, "I will do it. I would like to meet this boyar. Father, may I borrow your fishing net? I must fashion a dress from it."

The next morning she put on the fish net, took a dove in a cage and mounted a goat that was just the right size for her feet to drag on the ground. She half-rode, half-walked to the mansion of the boyar and, when he saw her arriving in this fashion, he ran out to meet her. Releasing the dove, which immediately flew away, she said, "My lord, there is your gift. Catch it for yourself."

The boyar was very impressed with the clever girl. "You are a smart one," he said. "I wonder if I should not marry you."

"And why not? I will marry you if you ask me," was her reply.

Right then and there it was settled. The old peasant had no objections, the daughter was pleased with the boyar, and the boyar was very much taken with the daughter.

The only problem that arose between them was that the boyar was afraid that the clever daughter was smarter than he was. He told her that she must not interfere in his affairs unless he asked for her advice. Most of the time that was not a problem, for the boyar was clever enough himself. He was just a little bit worried

that people would think his wife was the smarter of the two.

One day, two men came by to ask the boyar to solve their problem. One of them owned a mare, and the other owned the cart in which they were riding to the fair; the previous night the mare had had a foal, which they found under the cart. In the morning the cart-owner claimed the foal because it was under his cart, and the mare-owner claimed the foal because it was his mare. While they were bickering in the courtyard, the clever daughter heard them and came down to see what the trouble was.

When the problem was explained to her, she said, "This is something the boyar should properly handle, but he is not at home. He has gone to chase the fish from the grain."

"That is very strange! I have never heard of fish in the grain!" said one of the men.

"And I have never heard of a cart that could have a foal," she replied. "Obviously it was the mare that foaled."

When the boyar heard of this, he was very angry at his wife. "You were warned never to meddle in my affairs. Now you are no longer my wife. Tomorrow, you must go away. But, so people do not say I am unfair, I will allow you to take from this house whatever you value most."

That night, at their last supper together, she slipped a sleeping potion into his wine. After supper he lay down for his nap and passed out completely. The clever daughter called her two servants and told them to carry the boyar to the coach. They then drove to the home of the poor peasant, where the boyar was put to bed with the clever daughter. The peasant was fearful of the boyar, but he was very pleased with his daughter for her strength of character.

In the morning the boyar awoke and said to his wife, "What are you doing still here? I told you to go home."

"I am home," she replied. "It is you who are at my home. You told me to take whatever I value most, and I took you."

"Ay, ay, ay! You are indeed more clever than I am. I see I will have to forgive you and ask you to help me with all my decisions from now on. Come, let us return to *our* home."

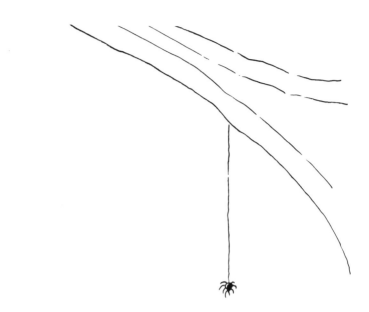

The Cossack and the Spider

A long time ago, during a fierce fight, there was a Cossack leader who fell in battle. He was seriously injured, and his men carried him to a quiet spot in a woods near the scene of the strife.

The Cossack sat with his back against a tree and tried to regain his strength. The situation seemed quite hopeless, as his men were badly outnumbered and the tide of battle was turning the way of the enemy.

As he sat and rested, he saw a spider that was trying to string a web from its tree to another tree a short distance away. The spider had just about reached the spot on the other tree where it wanted to fix its web, when it fell from the tree. Its thread kept it from hitting the ground, and it climbed back up to try again.

"What a marvellous thing is a spider," thought the Cossack. "It goes on spinning its web even though the world is collapsing around it."

He continued watching the spider. Each time the spider almost reached its goal, it fell. Instead of settling for another spot, the spider kept trying to reach the one it had chosen.

"Surely the spider will give up and go elsewhere," thought the Cossack. "That is now six times it has tried to reach its goal."

The spider did not quit. It made a mighty effort and finally succeeded. At this the Cossack took heart. "If a spider will not give up, there is no reason why I should be so weak," he thought.

The Cossack struggled to his feet and rejoined the battle, yelling with all his might to his men. When they saw him return, they took heart and surged forward, suddenly overwhelming their enemy. The battle was won!

For the lesson learned from a struggling spider, a victory was gained. If at first you do not succeed, try, try again.

The Cranberry Tree

Once upon a time there lived an old couple in a cottage on a hill near a large forest. They had two daughters who were as different in character as they could be. The older girl tended to be moody and grumpy, while the younger one was always lively and cheerful. In spite of their differences, they got along quite well together.

As the girls grew older, they often went to the forest to pick whatever berries were then in season. One day, they both went to the forest to pick berries and each came home with a full bowl. The older girl was not quite as careful in her picking; when their mother thanked them, she felt that those which her younger sister had picked were preferred. She became sulky and jealous of her sister.

A few days later, the girls again went to pick berries but, that afternoon, the oldest girl came home alone. She was upset because her

sister had wandered away and she could not find her. Both parents ran back to the forest with her and began looking for the lost girl. They called and called and searched everywhere, but there was no sign of her. Sorrowing and weeping, they made their way home, thinking that probably she had been seized by some wild animal.

The father never gave up looking for the lost girl. He often returned to the forest in the vain hope that he might find her still alive. One day, as he came to the spot where she used to pick berries, he saw something unusual. There was a cranberry tree growing there in the bush.

This surprised him, since he knew that such trees were not found in that area. This tree was of a nice trim shape and had the reddest berries he had ever seen. The old man played a sopilka, a kind of flute and, as his sopilka was getting old and cracked, he picked the straightest branch from this tree to make a new one.

He worked several days on his new sopilka. First the wood had to be properly dressed and cured, then it had to be hollowed and, finally, the holes had to be drilled. This last operation had to be done carefully and precisely. The holes had to be the exact proper distance apart, otherwise the notes would not be true.

When the sopilka was ready, he tested the notes and began to play a tune. To his surprise the music came out garbled, as if someone were trying to speak. He looked strangely at the sopilka and then blew strongly and steadily into it. The sopilka began to sing, and he made out the following words:

"Oh lowly, lowly,
My father, do play.
For my own cruel sister
Wickedly here did me slay.
With a knife through my heart
Did I from this world depart."

The old man dropped the sopilka on the ground when he heard this. He called to his wife, "Come quickly and listen to this!" She ran to him and, hearing the words, began to weep.

"Oh my God! What are we to do?" she cried.

"Let us wait till our daughter comes home," said the father. "I will play the sopilka and then we will hear what she has to say about this."

When the daughter came home, they asked her to tell them again what had happened to her sister. She became a little alarmed, but repeated the story she had told before.

The father then picked up the sopilka and began to play. The words came out clearly: "Oh, lowly, lowly." When the sopilka sang: "For my own cruel sister/Wickedly here did me slay," the girl turned pale and began to tremble. She fell upon her knees and told her parents how, in a fit of jealousy because her sister had filled her berry pail first, she stabbed her and buried her deep in the woods. Begging them to forgive her, she clasped her parents by the hands.

"Evil girl!" said the parents. "How can we forgive what you did? You both were our children and we loved you equally, but you, the elder, were always sullen and hard to get along with. If our neighbors hear of what you have done, you will be punished. You can no longer stay with us, for you will always be a reminder to us of your cruel deed. Go somewhere far, far away. We do not wish to see you any more."

Weeping, the girl packed her belongings and sorrowfully walked down the road. Coming to a curve, she turned for a last look at her old home. She saw the two old people with their arms about each other, slowly and sadly making their way into the house.

The Deceitful Nanny Goat

One morning, Dido went to market and bought a Nanny Goat. He took her home and sent his oldest son to take her to pasture. After she had spent a full day grazing by the stream, the boy drove the Nanny Goat home.

Just as they reached the gate, they saw Dido standing there in his red boots. Dido asked, "My darling little Nanny Goat, did you eat your fill, did you drink your fill?"

"No, Dido. I did not eat or drink," said the Nanny Goat. "On the way, I was able to grab only one maple leaf to eat and, when we crossed the dam, I could get only one drop of water. That is all I ate and drank all day."

Dido was angry at his son for neglecting his Nanny Goat and he sent him away from home.

Next morning, Dido sent his younger son out with the Nanny Goat. Again she spent the whole day grazing by the stream and, towards evening, the boy drove the Nanny Goat home.

When they reached the gate, they saw Dido standing there in his red boots. Dido asked, "My darling little Nanny Goat, did you eat your fill, did you drink your fill?"

"No, Dido. I did not eat or drink. On the way, I was able to grab only one maple leaf to eat and, when we crossed the dam, I could get only one drop of water. That is all I ate and drank all day."

Dido was angry at his son for neglecting his Nanny Goat, and he sent him away from home.

Next morning, Dido sent his wife with the Nanny Goat. Again the Nanny Goat spent the whole day grazing by the stream and, towards evening, Baba drove the Nanny Goat home.

When they reached the gate, they saw Dido standing there in his red boots. Dido asked, "My darling little Nanny Goat, did you eat your fill, did you drink your fill?"

"No, Dido. I did not eat or drink. On the way, I was able to grab only one maple leaf to eat and, when we crossed the dam, I could get only one drop of water. That is all I ate and drank all day."

Dido was very angry at his wife for neglecting his Nanny Goat, and he drove her away from home.

On the fourth day, Dido himself took his Nanny Goat to pasture. In the evening as he was driving her home, he ran ahead of her to the gate and stood there in his red boots. When the Nanny Goat arrived, he asked her, "My darling little Nanny Goat, did you eat your fill, did you drink your fill?"

"No, Dido. I did not eat or drink. On the way, I was able to grab only one maple leaf to eat and, when we crossed the dam, I could get only one drop of water. That is all I ate and drank all day."

At this Dido grew very angry. He had the blacksmith make a big long steel knife and he took the knife home to kill the Nanny Goat.

The Nanny Goat saw him coming with the knife and ran away. She ran and ran, through the bushes, through the brambles, and into the forest. There she found the home of a Rabbit. She ran in and hid on top of the pich.

When the Rabbit got home, he saw the open door and called out: "Who is in my hut?"

The Nanny Goat gruffly cried out:

"I am Demon Goat, for three coins bought!
With half my skin ripped,
On the thorns it was caught.
I will thump with my feet,
I will gore with my horns,
I will trample you down!
I will sweep you out with my tail
And with my chin-whiskers too,
And that will be the end of you!"

43

The Rabbit was so terrified that he ran away and sat weeping under a bush. A passing Bear heard the Rabbit crying and asked, "Why are you crying, little Brother?"

"How can I not cry? In my hut is a terrible beast who will kill me!"

The Bear said, "I am big and strong. I will drive the beast out for you."

Coming to the hut, the Bear said, "Who is in the hut of the little Rabbit?"

The Nanny Goat cried out:

"I am Demon Goat, for three coins bought!
With half my skin ripped,
On the thorns it was caught.
I will thump with my feet,
I will gore with my horns,
I will trample you down!
I will sweep you out with my tail
And with my chin-whiskers too,
And that will be the end of you!"

The Bear became frightened and said, "I am sorry, little Rabbit. I cannot chase the beast out. I am afraid of him."

The Rabbit again crept under the bush and cried. A Wolf heard the Rabbit crying and asked, "Why are you crying, little Brother?"

"How can I not cry? In my hut is a terrible beast who will kill me!"

The Wolf said, "I will drive this terrible beast out for you."

"Can you? The Bear was not able to do it."

"Just wait," said the Wolf. "You will see if I can drive him out."

Coming to the hut, the Wolf asked, "Who is in the hut of the little Rabbit?"

"I am Demon Goat, for three coins bought!
With half my skin ripped,
On the thorns it was caught.
I will thump with my feet,
I will gore with my horns,
I will trample you down!
I will sweep you out with my tail
And with my chin-whiskers too,
And that will be the end of you!"

The Wolf became frightened when he heard this. "No, little Brother Rabbit. I cannot do it. I am too afraid of him."

The Rabbit once again hid under the bush and cried. A Fox happened by and asked, "Why are you weeping, Brother Rabbit?"

"Oh, Sister Fox, there is an evil beast lurking in my hut!"

"I will drive the beast out," said the Fox.

"How do you think you can do it?" asked the Rabbit. "The Bear tried and the Wolf tried, but they could not do it."

"Just come and see," said the Fox.

45

The Fox went up to the hut and asked, "Who is in the hut of the little Rabbit?"

"I am Demon Goat, for three coins bought!
With half my skin ripped,
On the thorns it was caught.
I will thump with my feet,
I will gore with my horns,
I will trample you down!
I will sweep you out with my tail
And with my chin-whiskers too,
And that will be the end of you!"

The Fox became frightened and ran away. The Rabbit returned to his bush and wept again. Soon a Crab came by and said, "Why are you crying, little Brother?"

"How can I not cry? In my hut is a terrible beast who will kill me!"

The Crab said, "I will drive this terrible beast out for you."

"What? You?" said the Rabbit. "The Bear, the Wolf and the Fox tried, but they were too frightened and could not do it."

The Crab said, "Well, I can only try."

Coming to the hut, the Crab said, "Who is in the hut of the little Rabbit?"

Once more, the Nanny Goat yelled out in her most gruff voice:

"I am Demon Goat, for three coins bought!
With half my skin ripped,
On the thorns it was caught.
I will thump with my feet,
I will gore with my horns,
I will trample you down!
I will sweep you out with my tail
And with my chin-whiskers too,
And that will be the end of you!"

The Crab went into the hut, crept across the floor, and climbed up to the top of the pich, just behind the Goat. He said:

"I am just a poor Crab
Scuttling round in the dark,
But wherever I pinch
I leave a big mark!"

With that, the Crab nipped the Nanny Goat so hard that she bleated in pain. She jumped off the pich and ran out of the hut as fast as her legs could carry her. That was the last anyone saw of the terrible beast.

The delighted Rabbit thanked the Crab for chasing the beast away. He went into his hut and lived happily ever after.

The Enchanted Castle

Once upon a time, in a small village there lived a poor peasant. He owned no land, but he had a small cottage in which he lived with his family. His only means of earning his keep was as a hired laborer. It was hard to make a living, as he had a wife and three sons to support. When the boys grew old enough, they too had to go out to work.

As the boys grew older, they began to realize that there was not much of a future for them in their present situation. They talked the matter over and decided they would leave home. Discussing it with their parents, they said, "There is no hope of us ever making a living here. Let us go out into the world to seek our fortunes."

The parents agreed that something had to be done, but advised them not to all leave at once. "Perhaps it would be better if the eldest, Ivan, were to go first," suggested the father. "If

49

he is lucky and returns with something, then Josef will go. When he returns, Vasyl will try his luck. But remember, my children, to be honest and hard-working. For this, people will like you and the good Lord will bless your efforts."

The boys agreed and Ivan prepared for his journey. His mother baked a large loaf of bread for him, which he stuffed into his knapsack. Bidding everyone farewell, he departed.

Ivan walked one day, two days, and then a third day, but no one had any need for a laborer. Discouraged, he came at last to a large forest. He thought, "I will follow this path through the forest. Surely it must lead somewhere."

He was a little fearful, as there was a strong wind blowing through the trees, causing them to toss and mourn. Tired, he stopped by a well near the path. He drank some water and sat down under a large oak tree. He cut himself a piece of bread and began to eat.

Behind him, he heard a gentle mewing sound. He turned and saw a black cat walking towards him. "Here Kitsia," he called. "Are you hungry? Here is a piece of bread for you." The cat ate the bread and then spoke to Ivan.

"Thank you for your kindness," said the cat. "Where are you bound?"

Ivan was surprised to hear the cat speak, but tried to keep his excitement under control.

"I do not know myself where I am going," he replied. "I am just looking for work to earn myself some kind of a living."

"Well then," said the cat, "perhaps you would like to work for me."

"Certainly. Why not?" was the response.

"Fine. Then come with me. You will find the work very easy and the pay quite good."

They followed a path which led to a castle on the top of a mountain. It was a beautiful building surrounded by three rings of high walls.

"Here is where you begin your work," said the cat. "Everything in this castle is enchanted and under a heavy spell. One day in this castle will be equal to one year in your world. Your duties are simply to knock on the door of every room in the castle, calling, 'Glory be to Jesus Christ!'" So saying, the cat disappeared.

Looking around the courtyard, Ivan felt a great sadness, for nothing about him was living. There were many statues of people and animals, but they were all of stone and marble. Even the flowers were made of marble.

At first he was frightened by all the silence surrounding him, but he did have his duties to perform, so he began. He went from room to room, knocking on the doors and uttering the greeting. Each time he knocked and said the greeting a voice from inside would answer, "Glory be, forever!" He knocked on every door in the castle and on all the doors of the stables and the other buildings.

When the day ended and evening approached, he was met by the cat, who said to him, "You have been here for one whole year. Would you like to stay another year?"

Ivan replied that, although he would like that, he was unable to, as he had no more bread.

"Well then," said the cat, "since you are unable to continue, I will pay you. Go to the second wall around the castle. On the gate you will find a fine chain made of copper. Cut a piece as large as you can carry and sell it to a coppersmith in the first town on your way home. With the money, buy some land and you will be well-off. But I leave you with one warning: You must not tell anyone where you have been, nor how you got the chain, nor what you have seen."

Ivan promised to follow these instructions. He went to the gate, cut a large piece of the chain and left the castle. On the way home he sold the chain. With the money he received, he bought a comfortable piece of land. With this land and his toil, he became a successful farmer.

It was now time for Josef to go into the world and seek his fortune. As he was preparing to leave, Ivan suggested to his brother that he should take two loaves of bread, since he had found that one was not enough. Josef loaded his knapsack and departed with high hopes.

Like his brother before him, he could find no work near home. He followed the same path as his brother had done and met the same cat. He offered the cat some of his bread and was then just as surprised to hear the cat speak to him. He told the cat his story and the cat offered him the same work he had offered to Ivan.

Since Josef had two loaves of bread he was able to work twice as long as Ivan had done. After the second day, the cat gave Josef instructions to go to the first wall. On the gate he would find a silver chain. He was to cut as much as he could carry, sell the chain to a silversmith and buy himself some land. He also was warned not to tell anyone how he got the chain nor what he had seen at the castle.

Josef did as he was told. With the money he received for the chain, he bought some land with a nice house on it. With his hard work, he too became a successful farmer.

Now Vasyl had his turn. As he prepared to depart, Josef advised him to take three loaves of bread. With his knapsack stuffed full and his hopes soaring, Vasyl took his leave. He had the same success as his brothers. Meeting the cat, he offered it some of his bread. He, in turn, was offered the same work as his two brothers had done. With three loaves, though, he was able to contract to work for three days.

Vasyl passed the first two days uneventfully, knocking on all the doors and calling, "Glory be to Jesus Christ!" On the morning of the third day, however, as he knocked on a door, it suddenly opened. He found himself at the entrance to a large kitchen. A cook appeared and began to prepare a meal. He motioned Vasyl to a table and, with his finger to his lips, warned him not to speak. After eating breakfast, Vasyl continued his rounds.

Late in the morning, there began a great commotion all over the courtyard. Everything began to vibrate; the flowers became colorful and the statues returned to their living forms. Everything which had once lived and been turned to marble now regained its former state.

A beautiful girl approached Vasyl and said: "I am the owner of this castle. My parents died when I was very young. Having no one to guide me, I grew up to be a very proud and haughty person, with no kindness or mercy for anyone. One day while I was out for a walk, an old woman came to me. She greeted me politely and begged for alms, but I just turned her away and set the dogs on her.

"'You evil girl!' she shouted at me. 'May you be punished! You have a heart of stone, so may your castle and everything within be turned to stone! And you, my dear, the last one!'

"This terrible curse took effect at once. But God was merciful to me. He sent your brothers and you to this castle to save me. It was the spirit of my mother in the form of a cat who led you here. I thank God for His goodness to me and I thank you, Vasyl, from the bottom of my heart for helping to break this curse. I offer you all my possessions and my hand in marriage. Knowing my story, could you want me for your bride?"

"I am a poor, plain man," replied Vasyl, "and do not feel worthy of all this good fortune. However, it seems that this is the will of God, so I must accept. But I would like to return to my parents and bring them here to live with us."

The princess gladly agreed, and the two of them set out for the cottage of his parents. Since Vasyl had been away for three years, his parents were very happy to see him. They greeted his bride warmly and welcomed her. Soon the whole group travelled to the castle where Vasyl and the princess were married. They had a long and happy life and ruled their people well.

The Flying Ship

Once there lived an old peasant and an old woman with their three sons. The two older brothers were clever young men who could even borrow money without getting cheated, but the third was a very simple fellow named Ivan.

The parents treated the clever ones well. The old woman gave them clean white shirts and fed them well. But everyone scolded and laughed at the foolish son. He used to sit on the pich in a shabby shirt and tattered trousers. If he was given something to eat, he would eat it; if not, he went hungry. Sometimes they even forgot to feed him. But God loves simple folk, and he was a happy lad.

One day, there came a proclamation from the tsar saying that any man who could make a ship that could fly and would come with it to a feast he was giving at the palace would be given the hand of his daughter in marriage.

The clever sons were delighted. "We ought to go," they said. "Maybe we will be lucky and fortune will smile on us!"

They told their parents of their decision and asked for their blessing. Their mother gave them not only her blessing, but loaves of white bread, a roast pig and flagons of brandy for their trip. Their father gave them his blessing, along with much advice, and they set off.

Ivan watched these preparations. "I would like to go too," he said.

"You would never get there, you fool!" said his mother, laughing.

"The wolves would eat you as you stared at them!" said his father.

"They will not get me!" answered Ivan. "I want to go and I will go!"

The old people laughed at him at first, and then began to scold him, but he was determined. He kept saying; "I want to go and I will go! I want to go and I will go!"

When they saw that he would not change his mind they said, "All right, go then, go!" just to have a little bit of peace.

The old woman put some stale black bread and a flagon of water into a worn old sack and the old man saw him down the path. Ivan was sorry that he did not have such fine provisions as his two brothers had, but he was happy to be on his way to the palace of the tsar, where he was sure to get a fine dinner.

He walked and walked and sang merrily because he was so happy, until he met a gray-haired old grandfather with a long white beard and long white bushy eyebrows.

"Good day, Dido," said Ivan.

"Good day, son. Where are you off to?"

"To the palace for dinner," replied Ivan.

"Have you not heard that the tsar has offered the hand of his daughter in marriage to the man who brings him a flying ship?"

"And can you make a ship that can fly?"

"No," replied Ivan, "I cannot do that, for I do not know how."

"What are you going to do, then?"

"God knows," replied Ivan, "but I have nothing to lose. Perhaps I will be lucky and fortune will smile on me."

"In that case, you are not in a hurry," said the old man. "Let us sit down and rest, and we can have something to eat. What do you have there in your sack?"

"There is little here, Dido, except dry bread which is not fit to offer to guests."

"Never mind that. Take it out and let us eat what God has given."

Ivan looked in the sack only to find that the old crust of stale black bread had changed into such a loaf of fresh white bread and such a package of sliced meats that had never been seen before, except in the mansion of a boyar.

"Well, what is wrong?" asked the old man. "Have you nothing to drink at this meal? Maybe you have some brandy in your bag."

"Where would I get brandy from? I have only water in a flagon," replied Ivan.

"It will do then," the old man said.

Ivan took it out and tasted it. It had magically changed into brandy!

"Well now," the old man chuckled, "you see how God takes care of fools."

They sat down on the grass and ate their wonderful lunch. They ate and drank and sang songs besides, and had a happy time of it. When they were finished eating and making merry, the old man said to Ivan:

"Now listen carefully to me. Go to the forest. Cross yourself three times and hit the trunk of the first tree you see with your hatchet. Then quickly fall down flat on your face. Lie there until someone wakes you up. You will have a flying ship which will take you wherever you wish. But be sure to take with you every person you meet on the way."

The old man thanked Ivan for the lunch, and Ivan thanked the old man for his help. Then the old man went down the road and Ivan ran straight to the forest.

He went up to the first tree he saw, crossed himself three times and struck the trunk one blow with his hatchet. He then fell down flat on his face and went to sleep.

After a long time he thought he heard someone calling him, and he awoke. He stood up, and what did he see but a ship all finished and ready to go. Her masts were tall and straight, and her sails were made of silk and billowed in the wind. Ivan immediately climbed in and grabbed the tiller, at which the ship rose up and flew off. As the ship flew, it soared high over the trees, and Ivan steered along the road to the court of the tsar.

Noticing a man lying beside the road with his ear to the ground, Ivan flew down and called to him, "Good day, Vuiko!"

"Good day, Skyman!" was the reply.

"What are you doing?" asked Ivan.

"I am listening to everything that is happening in all the world."

"Then have you heard the proclamation of the tsar?" asked Ivan.

"Yes, I have."

"Are you going to the palace?" asked Ivan.

"Yes, I am."

"Come with me in the ship and I will take you there," said Ivan.

The Listener accepted the invitation and they flew off, singing songs and laughing. They flew and flew until they met a man hopping down the road on one foot with the other foot tied up to his ear.

"Good day to you, Vuiko!" said Ivan. "Why are you hopping along on one foot?"

"If I were to untie my other foot and take just one pace I would step across the whole world. But I do not want to do that just now."

"Where are you going, then?" asked Ivan.

"To the palace of the tsar."

"Come with us in the ship," said Ivan.

The Swift One joined them and they flew on together singing songs. They flew and flew until they saw an archer standing and taking aim with a bow and arrow.

Ivan called out, "Good day, Vuiko! What are you aiming at? There is nothing there."

"You mean you cannot see anything," replied the Archer. "Nothing is visible to you, but I can see much."

"Where do you see anything?"

"Ah," replied the Archer. "One hundred miles away a bird is sitting in a pear tree. Now, that is the kind of a shot that is worthwhile."

"Would you like to come with us to the palace of the tsar?" asked Ivan.

The Archer got in the ship and off they flew, singing louder and louder.

They flew on and on until they saw a man going by with a large basket of bread.

"Good day, Vuiko!" hollered Ivan.

"Good day, son!"

"Where are you going?" asked Ivan.

"I am going to get myself some bread for dinner," the man replied.

"But you already have with you a whole basket of bread!" exclaimed Ivan.

"This is nothing — it is only enough for a snack while I am on the road to get my real dinner," answered the Gobbler.

"Come with us to the palace of the tsar, and we will have a proper dinner," said Ivan.

The Gobbler accepted the invitation and off they flew. Their songs and their laughter rose to the sky as they went. They flew and flew until they met a man walking around a lake as though searching for something.

"Good day, Vuiko!" said Ivan.

"Good day to you."

"What are you looking for?" asked Ivan.

"I want a drink," he replied, "but I cannot find enough water."

"But there is a whole lake in front of you. Why do you not drink?"

"This drop? There is not enough here for one gulp," replied the Guzzler.

"Well, come with us!" offered Ivan.

The Guzzler accepted the invitation and they flew off singing and singing. They flew and flew until they saw below them a man who was carrying a sheaf of fresh straw.

"Good day, Vuiko!" called out Ivan.

"Good day to you, Man in the Sky!"

"Where are you taking that sheaf of straw?" asked Ivan.

"To the village."

"Is there no straw in the village?"

"Not like this."

"And what is different about this straw?"

"No matter how hot it is outside, as soon as I scatter this straw, frost and snow appear."

"There is a place for you with us in the ship," said Ivan.

The Straw-carrier sat down and they flew off once more, singing in chorus. They flew and flew until they met a man near the forest who was carrying a bundle of wood on his shoulders.

"Good day, Vuiko!" cried Ivan.

"Good day to you, too!"

"Where are you carrying that wood?"

"I am taking it to the forest."

"Is there no wood in the forest?" asked Ivan, with his eyebrows raised to his hair.

"Of course there is, but not like this," replied the Woodsman. "This is not common wood. If you scatter these sticks, immediately there will appear before your eyes a fully-equipped army of soldiers."

"Come and fly with us to the palace of the tsar," offered Ivan.

The Woodsman accepted the invitation and the ship flew on with its singing crew. They flew and flew and sang and sang until at last they arrived at the palace of the tsar.

In the middle of the courtyard there were many tables covered with linen and barrels of honey and wine were being rolled out. The tsar and his court were preparing for a huge feast. It seemed that half the world had come to the palace for dinner. Ivan and his companions in the ship anchored before the palace, got out of the ship and went to the feast.

The tsar heard the singing, looked out of his window and saw that someone had appeared in his courtyard in a flying ship. He called a footman to him and said, "Go and inquire of the great prince who has arrived in this flying ship."

The footman ran off and soon came back to the tsar. "A band of tattered muzhyks, peasants, came in the flying ship," he told the tsar.

The tsar did not believe him. "How can it be that poor muzhyks flew in such a ship? You probably did not make the proper inquiries."

The tsar went himself and asked the people, "Whose ship is this?"

Ivan stood up. "It is mine," he replied.

When the tsar looked at Ivan and saw his shirt covered with patches and his knees peeking through the holes in his trousers, he put his head in his hands and went back to the palace. "How can it be that I have promised the hand of my child to such a ragged muzhyk? What is to be done? I must set these peasants some impossible tasks, and they will be happy to get off with their lives."

"Go to the muzhyk who flew in the ship," he ordered his footman. "Tell him he must bring me some Water of Life from the Well at the End of the World before we finish feasting. If he cannot, I will not give the princess to him and my sword will remove his head from his body."

The footman set off to find Ivan. But the Listener had heard what the tsar said and had already told Ivan. Ivan sat on the bench and became so worried that he could not eat.

The Swift One came to Ivan and asked him, "Why do you not eat?"

"How can I eat?" asked Ivan. He told his friends what the tsar had ordered. "How can I bring Water of Life from the Well at the End of the World before the people finish feasting?"

"Ha! That is not a problem!" said the Swift One. "I shall get it for you."

Just then, the footman came to tell Ivan of the command of the tsar but, before the footman could speak, Ivan said, "Tell him I shall bring the Water." And the dumbfounded footman returned to report to the tsar.

The Swift One untied his foot from his ear, shook the stiffness out of his joints, and disappeared over the hill as soon as his foot hit the ground. After he had found the Well he was so tired that he said to himself, "The guests are still at the table and there is lots of time. I shall sit near this water mill and rest a little." He sat down and immediately fell asleep.

Meanwhile, in the courtyard, the tsar was finishing his dessert and the Swift One had not yet returned. Ivan sat down and thought to himself, "I shall lose my head for sure."

The Listener said he would try to find the Swift One. He put his ear to the ground and he listened and listened and finally he said, "He is snoring by the mill at the End of the World!"

"What are we to do?" asked Ivan. "How are we to waken him?"

The Archer spoke up then: "Fear not; I shall wake him up."

He raised his bow and shot one arrow. The arrow whacked the mill so hard that the Swift One jumped straight up in the air, and was back with the Water in no time at all.

The tsar was just finishing his cake when Ivan brought the Water to him.

Now the tsar had to think of another task to set before Ivan. Finally, he said to his footman, "The peasant and his friends must eat twelve roast oxen and forty ovens full of bread at one sitting." The Listener was listening and told Ivan what the tsar had said.

"Now what shall we do?" cried Ivan. "I cannot eat even one loaf of bread."

The Gobbler spoke up. "Why are you so worried?" he asked. "I shall eat everything, and it will not even be enough."

Before the footman could tell him of his next task Ivan said to him, "Bring on the oxen and the bread!" The bewildered footman returned to the tsar with this news.

The twelve roasted oxen and the forty ovens of bread were brought out. The Gobbler ate everything as fast as it appeared. "If only they would give me a decent meal," he complained. "Why are they so stingy?"

Then the tsar said to his footman, "Tell the muzhyk that he and his friends must drink forty barrels of beer in one sitting." The Listener told Ivan what the tsar had said and Ivan said, "Now, who is next to help us out?"

"I am," said the Guzzler. "I shall drink it all myself and ask for more." The servants brought in the forty barrels of beer and the Guzzler began to drink. He drank to the last drop and then he laughed. "This is not much," he said. "If I had a few barrels more, I might be happy."

The tsar thought to himself, "I must rid myself of that fool of a peasant somehow or he will ruin my daughter and my tsardom!"

He sent his footman to order Ivan to prepare for the wedding by bathing at the bathhouse. He commanded another servant to heat the cast-iron tub so hot that it was bright cherry-red. The servant heated the bathtub until it glowed from the heat.

The Listener told Ivan what to expect and, when he was summoned, Ivan went to the bath followed by the Straw-carrier. The bathhouse was so hot they could hardly get past the door.

The Straw-carrier scattered his straw and immediately it became so cold that they hardly had time to wash before the water froze solid. To keep warm, they climbed on top of the stove, where they sat singing songs and telling jokes until they both fell fast asleep.

In the morning when the servants opened the bathhouse door, there they were, snoring away on top of the stove. The servants ran to tell the tsar what they had found.

The tsar was very upset, and he tried once more to think how he could be rid of this man. Finally, he said to his footman, "This muzhyk must show me that he can defend his princess. Tell him he must come to me with a regiment of loyal armed soldiers." To himself, the tsar thought, "Where will a muzhyk like that get a regiment of armed soldiers? Only a prince could have that many men."

The Listener told this news to Ivan, who turned to the Woodsman and said, "Now you must show us what you can do."

The Woodsman replied, "I am only too happy to help my friends."

Soon, the footman came to Ivan but, before he could speak, Ivan said, "I shall appear before the tsar with two regiments of soldiers. But tell the tsar that if he does not accept me then, I will attack him and take not only his daughter, but also his crown and his tsardom!"

Then the Woodsman and Ivan went to the field and began to scatter the wood. Each stick turned into a hundred armed soldiers. Soon a huge army was assembled in the field, complete with cavalry and artillery.

The tsar was startled by the sudden sound of drums and trumpets. "Where is that music coming from?" he cried out.

"The army of the muzhyk who came in the flying ship," his footman said. "They are assembled outside the palace gate."

Despairing, the tsar at last summoned Ivan to the palace for an audience.

The lad who answered the summons was not the ragged fool the tsar had seen previously; now he was dressed as a general, and the gold of his helmet blazed in the sun. His uniform was decorated with medals and ribbons. He led his army, seated on a shiny black charger. Just behind him rode his friends, also in fine uniforms — the Listener, the Swift One, the Archer, the Gobbler, the Guzzler, the Straw-carrier and the Woodsman. They were all there.

The army entered the palace gate and halted in ranks. Ivan dismounted and crossed the courtyard. The astonished tsar embraced Ivan and kissed him on both cheeks.

The princess then came out and, when she saw Ivan, she smiled. What a handsome husband she would have! No matter if he was a fool — she was clever enough for two. And everyone knows that fools make the best husbands.

They were soon married and, at their wedding, there was such a feast that even the Gobbler and the Guzzler were satisfied.

The Frog Princess

There once was a tsar who had three sons, straight, tall and handsome. When the princes were of age, the tsar said: "My bright falcons, it is time you were married. Take your silver bows, go into the courtyard, and each of you shoot one copper arrow into the air. Where the arrows fall, there you will find your brides."

The three princes went into the courtyard and each shot an arrow. The arrow of the eldest flew to the clouds and landed in another tsardom, where a princess was walking in the palace garden. The arrow fell at her feet; she picked it up and took it to the tsar, her father.

"Look, Batko, I have found a copper arrow! What shall I do with it?"

Her father said, "Keep it until the owner comes to claim you as his bride."

The prince had followed his arrow on horseback. He entered the other tsardom, found the princess in her garden and said, "I have come here for my arrow."

The princess said, "No one shall have it but my husband-to-be."

The prince said, "I will most certainly have you for my bride."

Then and there they were betrothed, and the eldest prince rode home again.

Meanwhile, the second prince had shot his arrow into the sky. It flew over the trees into the courtyard of the castle of a duke. The daughter of the duke was sitting on the steps before the door. The arrow fell at her feet; she picked it up and took it to show her father.

"Look, Papa, I have found a copper arrow! What shall I do with it?"

The duke said, "Keep it until the owner comes to claim you as his bride."

The second prince had set out to follow his arrow. He came into the courtyard and found the lady sitting on the steps outside the door, holding his arrow. The prince said, "I have come for my arrow."

The daughter of the duke said, "No one shall have it but he who takes me for his bride."

The prince said, "I will most certainly have you for my bride."

They were betrothed and the second prince rode home again.

Meanwhile, the youngest prince, whose name was Ivan, had shot his arrow. It flew over the palace wall and landed in a swamp. Ivan went into the swamp after his arrow. On a mound in the middle of the swamp sat a green frog clasping the arrow in her damp arms.

Ivan said, "I have come for my arrow."

The frog replied, "I give it only to the one who takes me for his bride."

Ivan said nothing. He turned and went home, very troubled. What was he to do?

The tsar called the three princes before him and said, "Tell me, my bright falcons, of the brides you have found."

The eldest prince said, "I shall marry the daughter of a tsar."

The second prince said, "I shall marry the daughter of a duke."

Ivan hung his head and said nothing.

The tsar said, "Ivan, who is your bride?"

Ivan said, "What can I say? My brothers have found beautiful brides, but my copper arrow landed near a green frog in a swamp. What am I to do?"

The tsar said, "You must marry her, my son; I am afraid it is your fate."

The eldest prince rejoiced and married the princess. The second prince rejoiced and married the daughter of the duke. Ivan was married to the green frog; the frog rejoiced but Ivan did not.

The tsar gave each of his sons a palace to live in with their wives. One day he said: "I would like to see which of my daughters-in-law is the most skilled in matters of the home. Let each of them weave me a piece of cloth, and let them bring the cloth to me tomorrow morning."

That evening, at his palace, Ivan hung his head in sadness. The frog asked, "Ivan, my husband, why do you mourn?"

"How should I not mourn? My father bids each of his daughters-in-law to weave him a cloth. How could *you* weave a cloth?"

The frog said, "Do not worry. Go to bed and sleep. The morning is wiser than the evening."

Ivan went to bed and slept. His wife took off her frog skin to become a beautiful maiden, none more beautiful. She went into the courtyard and gave a whistle, and there appeared a loom. She snapped her fingers and skeins of colored silk appeared in her hands. She gathered up the thread, walked to the loom and quickly weaved the silk into the finest of cloth, emblazoned with eagles. She returned to the house, lay the cloth on the bed beside Ivan and put on her frog skin again.

In the morning, Ivan woke. There was the fine cloth, none finer in the world. He took it joyfully to the tsar, who said: "This is indeed beautiful! Never have I seen anything more beautiful! It shall hang on the back of my throne. The work of my other two daughters-in-law is fit only for the kitchen. Now let us see which of the three daughters-in-law can bake me the best cakes by the morning."

Ivan went home sadly.

The frog said, "Ivan, my husband, why do you hang your head?"

Ivan said, "How should I not? The tsar my father has bidden you to bake him some cakes. How can a frog bake cakes?"

The frog said, "Do not worry. Go to bed and sleep. The morning is wiser than the evening."

Ivan went to bed and slept.

The other two wives, meanwhile, were in conference. "What shall I do?" said one. "I have never baked a cake in my life!"

"Neither have I," said the other. "The frog surely must know what to do. Her weaving was beautiful. Let us watch her and see what she does. Then we will do the same."

They went to the palace where Ivan and the frog lived and, standing on tiptoe, peered in through the kitchen window.

The frog was on the table mixing batter. She mixed more and more water into the batter until it was thin and runny like soup. She climbed up and poured the batter on the hot stove. The batter bubbled and steamed and flowed all over.

The other two wives ran gleefully to their houses and did the same as the frog had done. They had a fine burnt mess for their efforts and were not able to present the tsar with any kind of a cake at all.

As soon as they were gone from the window, however, the frog took off her skin and became a beautiful maiden again. She whistled and the kitchen was instantly clean. She snapped her fingers and there appeared a large bowl of beautiful creamy batter. She put the batter in pans in the oven and, when the cakes were done, she took them out and arranged them on a silver tray. Then she put on her frog skin again.

In the morning when Ivan awoke, there were the cakes in a silver dish. Never had he seen such cakes! Joyfully he ran with them to the tsar. The tsar ate one, he ate two, then another and another. He ate all of them.

"These are the most delicious cakes ever!" he cried. "My other daughters-in-law made nothing. They cannot make cakes at all."

The next thing the tsar did was to announce a great banquet the next day, at which his three sons were to appear with their wives.

Ivan heard this and went home sadly.

The frog said, "Ivan, my sad husband, why do you frown so?"

Ivan replied: "How should I not frown? Tomorrow, the tsar is to give a banquet where we three sons must appear with our wives. How can I take *you* to a banquet, my frog? I shall be mocked by all the courtiers and all the guests!"

The frog said, "Do not worry, Ivan my husband, all will be well. You know that the morning is wiser than the evening."

Next day, as the time of the banquet neared, Ivan was very anxious. He had some hope, however, because the frog had made such beautiful cloth and such beautiful cakes; perhaps she could also make herself beautiful.

The frog told him: "Go on ahead, my husband. When the rain begins to fall, know that your wife is washing herself in raindrops. When you see lightning flash, know that your wife is dressing herself and, when you hear thunder roll, know that your wife is coming to you."

Ivan put on his finest clothes, mounted his horse and rode off to the banquet.

The brothers and their wives had already arrived. The brothers were richly clad and their wives were dressed in silk embroidered with gold and silver and diamonds.

The brothers mocked Ivan: "Well, Brother, have you come alone? Where is your wife? Could you not have brought her in your pocket or tied up in your lace handkerchief?"

"She will come soon," said Ivan.

Rain began to patter on the palace roof and Ivan, hearing it, said, "Now my dear wife is washing herself in the raindrops."

The brothers heard this and laughed. "Ivan, are you crazy?" they asked.

Lightning flashed and Ivan said, "Now my dear wife is dressing herself for the banquet."

The brothers looked at one another and shrugged. "Yes, he is mad," they whispered.

Then came such a tremendous clap of thunder that the whole palace shook. "Now my dear wife has arrived," said Ivan.

The words were scarcely out of his mouth when a glass coach drawn by eight fiery horses dashed into the palace yard. Out of the coach and up into the banquet hall stepped a princess so beautiful that everybody held their breath.

"She is so beautiful, it is not to be told!" whispered the tsar to the tsarina.

"Yes, so beautiful; her like is not on this earth!" replied the tsarina.

The tsar rose, led the beautiful princess to the table, seated her on his right hand and ordered the banquet to begin immediately.

The frog princess had a strange way with her. Every now and then, she would put a little bit of food in her right sleeve and, every now and then, she would put a little drop of wine in her left sleeve. The other two wives watched and copied her; they put a bit of food in the right sleeve and a drop of wine in the left sleeve. It did not seem to be a particularly pleasant thing to do, but they were not going to be outdone by a frog, even if she had turned into a princess more beautiful than the sun.

When the feast was over, they all proceeded to the courtyard where music was playing. The dance was about to begin.

The tsar said, "Let my sons and their wives lead out the dance."

The wives of the two elder brothers said, "Let Ivan and his wife dance first." They thought: "Even if she is lovely, she was born in a swamp; how should she learn to dance? Now perhaps she will stop putting us to shame."

Ivan and his wife led out the dance. The frog princess moved so beautifully and so lightly that her feet scarcely seemed to touch the floor. Everyone stood and stared. Surely never since the world began had there been such dancing!

By and by, the frog princess bade Ivan sit down, for she wished to dance by herself. Off she went, skimming over the floor like a swallow over a pond. She waved her right sleeve and a little something fell out of it. The little something turned into a garden. In the middle of the garden stood a pillar and on the pillar sat a white cat. When the cat ran down the pillar, he sang songs and, when he ran up, he told stories.

Off went the princess again, skimming the ground like a swallow. She waved her left sleeve and there appeared in the garden a river with twelve white swans swimming. The company watched breathlessly and, when the princess sat down to rest, the courtyard echoed with cheers.

"Now let my other two daughters-in-law dance!" cried the tsar.

The other two wives got up to dance, though they did not much want to. They danced and whirled and twirled. They were doing their best, but the tsar was not entranced. One daughter-in-law waved her right sleeve and a chicken bone flew out of it and landed on the ground in front of the tsar. The other daughter-in-law waved her left sleeve and a portion of wine flew at the tsar.

"Enough, enough!" cried the tsar. "Stop before you drown me! Take your partners and let everyone dance."

The music played joyfully and everybody danced and danced, while the frog princess sat beside the tsar and watched.

Ivan sneaked away from the dance, ran to the stable, jumped on his horse and galloped back to his own palace. Could that wonderful princess really be his wife, or would he find his frog still at home?

Up into her bedroom he ran; there on the bed, he saw a green frog skin. "Oh, my wife, my beautiful one!" he cried. "Never, never shall you have to be a frog again!" He grabbed the frog skin and threw it into the fire, burning it up, then rode back to the dance.

At dawn, the party ended and Ivan went home with his wife. She looked into her bedroom and asked, "Where is my garment?"

Ivan said, "If you mean that awful green frog skin, I have burned it."

"Alas!" she cried. "Ivan, my Ivan, what have you done? Without my skin, I cannot remain here. Search for me on the Mountain of Glass, if ever you find it. Goodbye, my Ivan."

She waved her hand, turned into a cuckoo and flew out of the window.

Ivan wasted no time. He ran to the stable, leaped on his horse and galloped off. He did not know where he was going, but find his princess again he must, and would.

He rode and rode, asking all he met if they could tell him of the Mountain of Glass, but no one knew of it. Finally, one day, very tired and near despair, he met up with a little old man who was as white as milk.

"Whither away, my friend?" asked the little old man of Ivan.

"I am seeking my wife on the Mountain of Glass. Do you know, Dido, where it may be?"

"How should I not? Certainly I know!"

"Then please tell me, tell me!"

"Why should I tell you, my son? It would do you no good, for I think you would never arrive there. It would take the bravest man in the world to reach that mountain. Go home, my son, and live your life in safety."

Ivan drew his sword. "Will you tell me, Dido, or will I cut off your head?"

The little old man laughed, "I see you have a stout heart." He took a ball out of his pocket and, giving it to Ivan, said: "Drop this ball on the ground before you and follow where it leads. It will show you the way to the Mountain of Glass that stands at the end of the world."

Ivan thanked the old man, took the ball, and threw it before him. Off rolled the ball and after it galloped Ivan. Over hill, over dale, through forest, bog and fen he rode, till he came to the end of the world. There, towering up into the sky before him, rose the Mountain of Glass. Around the mountain flowed a great river; over the river stretched a narrow bridge; beyond the bridge stood three giants keeping guard. The ball stopped rolling; it would not cross the bridge.

Ivan was about to gallop over the bridge when there, barring his way, stood the little old man as white as milk.

"Stop, stop! Do you not see the giants?"

"Yes, I see them. What of it?"

"There is this of it," said the little old man. "If you cross the bridge now, they will tear you limb from limb and eat you mouthful by mouthful. Will that save your princess?"

"But I must save her, and I will!"

"Then wait, impatient fellow!" said the little old man. "At sunset, the giants will lie down to sleep and then you may cross. Take these four cloths and wrap them about the hooves of your horse, lest by his clattering on the bridge he wake the giants before you have passed them. As soon as you have passed, the giants will wake and start after you. Here is a packet of dust. When the giants come, throw the dust behind you. The dust will fill the air and the giants will see nothing, and so you will be able to escape.

"Beyond the river you will find a mill; ask the miller for lodging. At supper the cook will bring the miller a roast cockerel. He will eat it all himself, refusing you even a morsel. The bones of the cockerel he will order his cook to burn in the fire. You must give her a piece of gold and she will hide them for you. When the miller is asleep, be off with you to the Mountain of Glass, taking the bones with you. Throw them at the mountain one after the other and they will make steps for you to climb by. At the top of the mountain you will meet the witch, Old Bony-Legs. Remember your manners, Ivan, and do not anger her. She holds the safety of your wife in her hands. And so farewell to you, Ivan. In this world we shall never meet again."

Ivan had scarcely time to thank the old man before he vanished.

Ivan bound the cloths around the hooves of his horse and waited till sunset. When the giants lay down to sleep, Ivan crossed the bridge; the cloth-bound hooves made no sound. Nevertheless, the giants started up the moment he had passed them. He shook the dust out of the packet and, though it was still day before him, it was night behind. The giants stumbled about in the darkness, seeking but not finding.

Ivan rode on and came to a mill. He said to the miller, "I seek lodging for the night."

The miller barred the door and said, "I give lodging to no common man."

Ivan said, "I am a prince; I am able to pay you quite handsomely."

Hearing this, the miller invited him into the mill and they sat down to dinner.

The two ate a good dinner and then, towards the end of their meal, the cook brought in a serving dish with a roasted cockerel in it.

"You eat none of this," said the miller to Ivan. "This is *my* dish!"

He gobbled up the whole cockerel and bade the cook burn the bones in the fire.

Before the cook could burn the bones, however, Ivan quietly gave her a piece of gold and she hid the bones in her apron. When the miller had gone to bed and was soundly snoring, she took the bones to Ivan.

"What good they may do you is none of my business," she said, "but the piece of gold is."

Ivan took the bones and rode off to the Mountain of Glass. He threw one bone at the mountain and there appeared a step. He climbed up onto that step and threw another bone. Another step appeared. He carried on throwing the bones before him and the bones carried on making steps until, at sunrise, he reached the top of the mountain.

There, he saw a great glass castle. At the door of the castle stood the witch, Old Bony-Legs.

"Ah, a handsome young man!" cried Old Bony-Legs. "Come in, my precious! Tell me, None-So-Handsome, what do you want of me?"

Ivan bowed low. "I have come for my princess, my dear wife."

"Well, well, I will give her to you but, first, you must do me a little service."

"I will gladly serve you," said Ivan.

Old Bony-Legs took him to a garden behind the castle, where there was a big pond. "I have been waiting for years to have the pond bailed dry," she said. "Empty it for me and you shall have your princess. Here is your bailer."

She gave Ivan a thimble with a hole in it. "If the pond is dry by sunset, well and good. If not, I shall have to cook you and eat you for my supper, None-So-Handsome."

She left him holding the thimble and went back to her castle screeching with laughter.

Ivan threw the thimble into the pond and began to bail out the water with his cupped hands. The hours went by and, the more water he bailed out, the more the pond filled. The sun was going down in the sky and would soon set. He would never empty the pond, he would never win back his princess, and Old Bony-Legs would have him for her supper.

Ivan flung himself down and wept.

"Ivan, my husband, why do you weep?"

Ivan sprang to his feet. "My love, my beautiful one, my princess!"

It was indeed his princess.

The princess waved her hand over the pond and the pond was dry!

"Now we are saved!" cried Ivan. "Come, let us go from here, quickly, quickly!"

"Not yet," said the princess. "We still have to deal with the witch, who has held me in her power these many years. When she finds the pond dry, she will take the shape of a rain cloud, a huge, dark cloud. Draw your sword, Ivan and, when that cloud comes, as come it will, look well at it and strike where the darkness is thickest."

Scarcely had the princess spoken when a great darkness rushed from the castle. It was all black, but darkest near the ground, and there Ivan struck with his sword. The darkness screamed, the darkness vanished, and there lay Old Bony-Legs, pierced through the heart.

The princess turned herself into a cuckoo, took Ivan under her wing and flew with him down from the mountain, past the mill, over the heads of the giants and across the bridge. There she set him down, turned back into her own beautiful shape and whistled loudly.

Ivan saw his horse who, when he heard the whistle, came galloping to them. Ivan and the princess rode to their home, where they lived happily, none more happily, for ever after.

The Gossip

Ivan and Marusia were peasants who lived in a hut on the edge of the land belonging to their landlord. One day, Ivan was in the woods checking his traps when he stumbled across a chest full of gold coins. He was delighted at first, and then crestfallen. "How can I keep this money? If the landlord hears of it he will claim it as his own, and how can he not hear of it when my Marusia is the biggest gossip on this earth? She talks of everything to everyone and when there is nothing to talk of she talks of that, too. With a wife who has a tongue that flaps continually like washing on a line, I must be very careful how I handle this."

He buried the treasure and went to check his traps as he thought about his problem. One trap had a rabbit in it, which he put into his bag. Still thinking, he went to the river to check his fish net. As he was pulling a large pike out of the net, he was struck with an idea. He put the fish in his bag and left the rabbit in the net. Then he went back to the forest and put the fish in the rabbit trap. He then went home.

"Marusia!" he called when he got home. "Cook us up some pancakes. I have found a chest of gold in the woods, and we must build up our strength if we are to carry it home."

Marusia was so excited that she trembled as she made the pancakes. Her mind was whirling with plans for the money. Wait till her sister-in-law heard about this! She was so preoccupied with her own thoughts that she did not notice Ivan piling the pancakes into his bag.

"How hungry you are, my dear!" she exclaimed. "It is good that you found the money, for you are eating everything in the house!"

Finally, dusk arrived and the two went off to get the treasure. Marusia prattled away about their good fortune as she made her way through the woods behind Ivan. He was just far enough ahead that he could hang pancakes all over the trees without her seeing. Finally, she hollered at him and he stopped and turned.

"Come see," she said. "There are pancakes hanging in all these trees!"

"Oh, yes," he said. "Did you not see the pancake cloud that passed over us just now? It rained pancakes, and we were lucky that it was not a shower large enough to suffocate us."

As excited as she was about the treasure, Marusia now began to babble away about the wonderful pancake cloud. On the way, they stopped at a rabbit trap, and there was the large pike stuck in it.

"Oh ho! What is this?" she exclaimed. "I have never seen a fish caught in a rabbit trap!"

"And now you have," was the reply. "It is nothing more than a land pike."

They then passed the river, where Ivan pulled in his net. When she saw the rabbit in the net, Marusia could not believe her eyes. "What is this? I have never seen a rabbit in a fish net!"

"Now you have," said Ivan. "It is nothing but a little river rabbit."

Finally, they arrived at the treasure. Ivan dug it up and put the coins in his bag, and they headed for home. As they were walking, they could hear a great ruckus from the village alehouse where some drunks were fighting.

"Good gracious, Ivan! What is the row all about? I must go see!"

Ivan stopped her. "Leave evil things alone. The steward of the landlord stole some sausages today and he is being punished in public. The landlord has him in the alehouse and is beating him with a large ring of kobasa. Let us avoid trouble and go to bed. And be sure that you do not mention to anyone the events of tonight, or things will go badly for us."

It was a strange night for Marusia and she barely slept with the excitement of it all. In the morning, she was up at dawn, counting the money. Shortly after daybreak, she was at the village well, waiting for someone to tell the story of their good fortune. By breakfast-time, the whole village knew of the gold and, soon after, the landlord summoned Ivan and Marusia to appear at his manor.

"What is this I hear about you with some gold that rightfully belongs to me?" he asked.

Before Ivan could say anything, Marusia blurted out, "Oh please, sir. We did not know it was yours. What with all the excitement of the pancake cloud and the river rabbit and the land pike, we must have become confused."

The startled landlord looked at Ivan, who shrugged his shoulders as if to say, "I do not know what she is talking about!"

Turning to Marusia, the landlord told her to tell him the whole story, which she did. She told him everything, including the story of the steward and the sausages. The landlord grew redder and redder. Finally, he exploded. "How dare you waste my time with this nonsense? Get out of my sight!"

"Does that mean we can keep the treasure?" asked Marusia.

"Yes, and the pancakes and the river rabbits and all the rest of it, too! Now get out!"

On the way home, Marusia mulled over what had happened. Then, when Ivan finally burst out laughing, she was very, very angry. "Look what you made me do!" she yelled at him. "Now everyone will think I am nothing but a crazy old woman!"

"I did not make you do anything," said Ivan. "I told you to say nothing, but you could not do that. You brought it all on yourself."

They talked it over and forgave each other, and Marusia resolved not to gossip any more. But that did not matter, because nobody listened to her any more anyway.

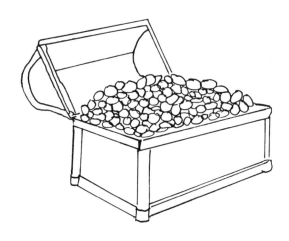

The Little Golden Harp

Many many years ago, in ancient times, there lived three kings in the lands of the Far East. They were not ordinary kings, but very learned men who studied the heavens and all the stars. There were no books in those days, but they knew how to read the marks that had been scratched on clay tablets by other wise men. They would talk to old men who lived alone in caves and in the desert. These old men were sages, or seers, who could foretell the future.

The three kings were named Melchior, Caspar and Balthazar. Since their kingdoms were not far apart, they would meet to discuss the things they had learned or observed.

At one of these meetings, Melchior reported that an old sage had told him about the forthcoming birth of a king. This king was to be a very different kind of ruler than they were. He was to be the King of the World. The sign of his birth would be the appearance of a bright new star in the heavens, which would guide worshippers to the place of his birth. The three kings agreed that, when the star appeared, they would make the journey to greet the new king and offer him gifts.

Melchior had a young daughter named Lelia. She was very pretty, like a flower but, unfortunately, she was unable to speak. When she was six years old, a lion had somehow found its way into the palace grounds and frightened her so badly that she lost her power of speech. Melchior had many doctors try to cure Lelia, but they were unable to do so. Although she could not express herself in words, she loved music and spent much of her time with the musicians and singers. The king had his craftsmen make a little golden harp for her and she spent many happy days playing it.

One night, a star brighter than any other appeared in the sky. This was the sign Melchior had been waiting for and he began preparations for the journey. He sent messengers to Caspar and Balthazar, and all three met, each with his own attendants, supplies and armed guard.

As Melchior was gathering the gifts for the newborn king, Lelia came and put her golden harp in with the other items. By signs, she made Melchior understand that she wished to give it to the child as her own gift.

The journey was not an easy one. It was long and there were deserts and rivers to cross. They passed through storms and, at times, had to fight off bands of robbers who attacked them.

The star led them to the country of Judea where they stopped near a little town at the foot of a hill. As Judea was at this time ruled by King Herod, the three kings left their camp and went to Herod to pay their respects to him.

Herod was very interested in their news. He wanted to know exactly where the new king was born. Since they did not know, they were unable to tell him. He then asked them to be certain to inform him when they found the child, as he too wanted to worship this newborn king.

The kings returned to their camp in the hills and waited for the star to appear again. That night, the star led them to the little town of Bethlehem and to a stable beside an inn. This greatly surprised the kings; they expected a king to be born in a palace, not a stable.

Looking at each other, they nevertheless went into the stable. There was a curious light inside which was illuminating a little Baby in a manger. Mary and Joseph were standing beside Him. The kings fell to their knees and bowed to Him, presenting their gifts of gold, myrrh and incense. Melchior presented the golden harp from Lelia and laid it beside the Child. Little Jesus was waving His arms and kicking His legs, and His hand brushed against the strings of the harp. A wonderful melodious sound of music filled the stable and made Melchior very happy.

That night in camp, an angel appeared to Melchior in a dream. The angel warned him that Herod was evil and wished to kill the child. He told him to leave Judea as quickly as possible and to take a different route home. Melchior woke the others and they quickly made their way far beyond the borders of Judea.

Melchior was soon at his own home. While walking into his palace, he heard a child with a clear ringing voice singing in the orchard. The child was singing, "In the manger on the hay, a child is resting and for him my harp did play." Hardly believing what he had heard, he realized that it was Lelia singing.

Meeting with his family, Melchior asked for the exact time when Lelia had regained her speech. The queen told him that on a certain night at a certain time, Lelia had clapped her little hands and cried out, "Mama, Mama! I can talk!" Melchior then realized that this had happened at the exact moment when Baby Jesus had struck the little golden harp with His hands.

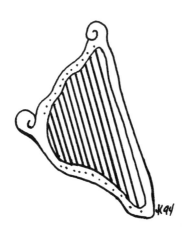

The Poplar and
the Greedy Woman

Nykola was a poor old peasant who lived in a cottage in the woods with his wife Eufemia. They lived a simple, happy life.

One fine day, Nykola said, "I will go to the forest and chop some wood for the winter." He lifted his axe to his shoulder and set off.

He chose a fine old poplar tree and had just raised his axe to strike when he heard the tree speak. "Do not cut me down, my good man," it said. "I can be of use to you."

Nykola was so startled that he dropped his axe and stood there petrified. Finally he took heart and haltingly asked, "Does a tree speak with a human voice?"

"I do. I am an unfortunate enchanted tree and I feel pain like a human does. It would be as bad for me to die as it would be for you to die."

"Well then, and you shall not die by my hand," Nykola said.

"You have given me my life," said the tree. "Now what can I give to you?"

Nykola sat down and thought and thought. "Poplar," he said finally, "I cannot think of anything that I need that I do not have."

"If ever you do think of something," the tree said, "come and ask."

Nykola picked up his axe and went home. He would not cut trees in that part of the forest again. When he got home, his wife asked him where the wood for winter was. He told her what had happened, and she was angry with him.

"You are nothing but a fool," she said. "Go back and tell the tree you want some bread. I hope it is not too late to ask the tree for this."

"Yes, my dear," replied Nykola. He put on his cap and went to the forest. When he came to the tree he said, "Poplar, please be so kind as to give my wife Eufemia some bread."

"It is done," said the poplar. "Go home."

When Nykola got home, Eufemia was shouting and dancing. "You should see! There has never been so fine a loaf of bread!" She led him into the cottage and, there on the table, was a huge loaf of fine white bread. "My husband, you have not done so badly, after all."

That night, the old woman woke Nykola and said, "I have been thinking. If it was so easy for the poplar tree to give us some bread, tomorrow you must go back and ask for a horse and cart. Let us see if he can do that."

In the morning, after a breakfast of fine bread, Nykola got his cap and went back to the poplar. "I beg your pardon," he said, "but could you please give my wife a horse and cart?"

"It is done," said the poplar. "Go home."

When he got home, there in front of the house were a horse and cart, and Eufemia was sitting in the cart with a big smile on her face.

"Look, husband," said the old woman. "Now we are real people! But such a cart and horse make our tumbledown house look even more shabby. Go to the tree and ask for a new house."

"I am not sure I want to do that," he said.

"Go on," she said. "The cart and horse were easy for him, and he does owe his life to you."

"That is true, but I do not like to bother him too much." Still, the old man went to the poplar tree and said, "My wife is very pleased with the bread and the horse and cart, but she would like to have a better house to live in."

"It is done," said the poplar. "Go home."

When the old man came into his yard, he did not recognize anything. In the spot where the humble old cottage had been, there was a beautiful new house. The old woman was skipping for joy like a child. You would think that now she would be happy.

Instead, she said to Nykola, "I am tired of being a poor peasant. Go tell the tree that we want money and we want to be boyars. People must bow when they come near. We must have servants to do our work, and they must fear us."

The old man went to the poplar tree and asked for all of this for his wife.

"It is done," said the poplar. "Go home."

When Nykola got home, he found his wife counting piles of gold coins. There were servants and guards everywhere. He stood there silently and sadly, and she said to him: "Would it not be wonderful if the whole village worked for us as our servants? Then we could be content and live peacefully the rest of our days. Go and tell the tree that this is what we really want."

Nykola returned to the tree one more time and told it what his wife wanted now. The poplar was silent, and Nykola repeated his request. Finally the poplar said, "One last favor shall be done for you, my friend. Go home."

When Nykola got home, he found his old wife standing beside their old cottage. Everything else was gone — the servants, the new house, the horse and cart, even the last crust of the big loaf of bread. All that remained was the old woman standing by the cottage.

Nykola was overjoyed to see everything as he had remembered it. The old couple resumed their old life and Nykola grew happier and happier as time went on. Eufemia never mentioned another word about wanting anything she did not have.

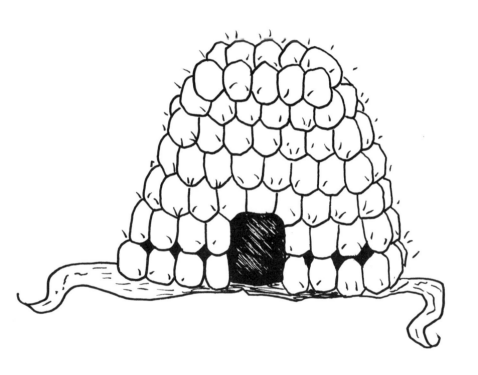

The Raspberry Hut

In a country far across the sea, there once lived a poor cottager who owned no land other than that upon which his cottage stood. He supported his wife and son by working for other people. Being an honest and hard-working man, he was never idle.

One summer there was a long period of hot, dry weather. Then, at last, the heat ended. The sky turned gloomy and black clouds rolled in, bringing with them a terrific storm. Heavy rains came down and the rivers and creeks overflowed their banks, flooding the countryside. With a roar, the wild waters rushed over the fields and meadows surrounding the village near which the cottager lived. Trees were uprooted, cattle were drowned and homes were destroyed.

One afternoon shortly after the storm, the cottager walked over to the edge of the river which flowed past his home. He watched the wild waters for a while and then, to his horror, saw a cradle with a baby in it floating by. The child was crying and reaching out as if begging for help. The man did not think twice but jumped into the water and swam towards the cradle. Just as he reached out for it, a large tree, carried by the rushing waters, struck him a heavy blow and he sank out of sight.

Soon a large crowd of neighbors gathered at the cottage, hearing the wailing of his poor wife. Her weeping and lamenting for her lost husband touched everyone.

Through the crowd, a stranger made his way up the path and said: "Woman, do not weep! God gave you a good husband and God took him away. Let His will be done. Remember that you still have a son to bring up. You must see that he grows up to be a good, useful man. Pray to God for mercy and help in your misfortune. He will not let you down."

Hearing this, the poor widow fell to her knees and prayed as the stranger turned and disappeared into the crowd.

The woman went back into her cottage and said to her son: "Andriy, your father is no more! He has gone to be with God and will never return. There will be no one to work and earn our keep. Let us pray to God and beg Him to bless you so that you will grow to be an upright man and be a comfort to me in my old age."

The good Lord did not abandon the widow and her son. The village priest spoke to the people and they all promised to help. The rich landlady who owned the village and all the fields around it sent food and money to the bereaved woman. The other villagers helped as they were able. The widow thanked them all but did not remain idle. With the produce of her garden and by doing jobs for others, she worked hard to earn enough money to pay for her needs. Even little Andriy helped by selling the berries he picked in a nearby forest.

One day the next summer, it was calm and hot. It seemed that the very breeze had gone to sleep. Andriy was picking raspberries in the forest. Feeling very tired, he found a cool spot under an oak tree and fell asleep.

He had not slept very long when he was awakened by the twittering of a bird just above him. Andriy rubbed his eyes and watched. He had never seen a bird with such beautiful feathers before. It flitted over to another tree. Getting up, Andriy followed the bird to the next tree, then to the next and the next and the next. Before long, he found himself deep in the forest. Reaching a glade, he spied something red in a little clearing. It was an odd thing; it looked like some sort of a large fruit.

He ran towards the object. To his surprise, he realized that it was a huge raspberry, bigger than his cottage. It made his mouth water, so he pulled out his knife to cut off a piece to eat. As soon as he stuck the knife in it, the berry opened up and he found himself in a bright room. The raspberry was, in fact, a large hut.

A door opened and a man stepped into the room. It was the stranger who had walked up to the cottage the day Andriy had lost his father.

"Do not be afraid, Andriy," said the man. "Nothing bad will happen to you. Thank God that He made me your guardian. Always be polite, obedient and diligent and all will be well with you. I will teach you many good and worthwhile things if you stay with me and be my student."

"I would be very glad to stay with you," said Andriy, "but my mother will be worried if I do not come home."

"Do not worry about that. I will let her know that you are here with me," said the man. "You just look around here in this room while I prepare lunch. You must be hungry." Having said that, the man went into another room.

Andriy began looking around. There were many toys that he had never seen before nor even dreamed of. The shelves were loaded with books but, since Andriy could not read, he only looked at the many pictures in them. It was like a new world opening up for him.

After a while, when Andriy had eaten lunch, the man told him of his plans: "You will stay with me for fourteen days. Promise to study very hard and get all the education possible, for only then can you become a successful man. You must also understand about time in my world, as it is very different from yours. Each day you spend here will be like one year in your world. So, Andriy, what do you say to that?"

All Andriy could do was thank the man for his kind offer and promise to do his best. He kept his word and studied very hard during his stay at the Raspberry Hut. As time progressed, he grew to be a handsome youth and, finally, his days and years of studies drew to a close.

When the fourteenth day arrived, he fell into a sort of trance. The hut had risen and was floating through the air. It crossed the countryside and hovered above a large city. Everything on the ground looked so small. Even the people looked like ants crawling around.

"Is it true? Are we really floating above a large city?" asked Andriy.

"Yes, it is true. We are over the capital city of your country, which is ruled by a very good prince. Unfortunately, he is extremely ill at present and no doctor seems able to cure him. The people are very sad because he is a just and a good ruler. But I know how to cure him," said the man. From his case he took a vial into which he mixed some medicine which he gave to Andriy. "Take this and, before you give it to the prince, mix it with water. He will become well."

The man continued: "You have been with me for fourteen years. You grew up and received an education like no other person on earth. Now the time has come for you to return to your own world. I am but a spirit and must leave you. My role is to take care of worthy orphans like you.

"Now let me give you some parting advice. Always be pious and honest, and be kind and helpful to those in need. When someone does you wrong, repay them with good; that way you will convert your enemies to friends. Be fair and just and consider all your actions carefully before carrying them out.

"Go to the palace now and cure the prince. He will reward you well. Farewell!" The hut gently landed in a wooded park. Andriy thanked his teacher and stepped out, and the hut immediately rose into the air and disappeared.

Andriy walked to the gates of the castle where a guard stopped him. "Who are you and what do you want?" the guard asked.

"My name is Andriy and I have come to cure our prince, who is very ill," was the reply.

The guard stared at him and said, "We have had all the best doctors in the country and they could not help him. Who do you think you are and what makes you think you can do it?"

The chamberlain of the court, who was nearby and had overheard this conversation, approached and said: "The prince is very low and may not survive much longer, so we will take a chance with this young man. I will take him into the castle with me. Let us hope that he is right."

"God willing, I can cure him," Andriy said. "Take me to him and you will see for yourself whether I will be able to help him or not."

The prince was very ill indeed. He barely stirred when they entered his room. Quickly mixing the potion, Andriy gave the prince a sip of it. In a few minutes, the prince breathed easier and fell asleep. The next morning, for the first time in his long illness, he asked for food. From then, on his health improved rapidly. Once the prince found that his savior was a well-educated man, he kept Andriy in his court. He listened to many of his suggestions and came to rely on his abilities and his judgment.

One event occurred which proved that Andriy had some knowledge of the more serious matters of life in those times. The neighboring boyar was a greedy sort and, hearing of the illness of the good prince, decided to take this opportunity to attack him and seize some of his lands. He had little respect for the generals or the army of the prince. However, when he invaded the country, he met unexpected resistance. Andriy led the army against him and proved to be an able leader. After a long and fierce battle, the enemy was defeated. The evil boyar lost not only the war but also the territories he had taken in previous wars.

The prince and all his people were happy with the victory, since it ensured peace for a long time to come. Having no heir, the prince announced that Andriy would be the eventual successor to the throne.

Even with all these honors heaped upon him, Andriy did not forget his mother. He prepared for the journey home and, one day, set out for his village. His mother greeted him happily, as she had not seen him for many years.

After visiting with her and the neighbors, he coaxed his mother into returning to the city with him. She finally agreed but, after staying with him only a few days, she asked to be returned to her home. She said that she was not used to all the finery and the hustle and bustle of a large city. Besides, she missed her friends in her village. She lived long enough to see her son become the ruler after the passing of the prince.

Andriy ruled his people wisely and justly for many, many years.

The Raven

In one old country in Europe, there still can be seen the remains of an ancient castle. On one side of the ruins there is a forest and, on the other side, a village. Travellers still ask about the castle and how it came to be destroyed.

The villagers tell the story of how it was built a very long time ago by a rich knight who was a baron. He and his family were very evil and kept a large band of brigands with whom they oppressed their neighbors. They forced the villagers to work for them and to pay high taxes. They attacked weaker neighboring landowners and robbed them. They were cursed by all their neighbors, who hoped that some day this nest of scoundrels would be destroyed.

Such an event came about one day. The tsar, having heard of the evil doings, invaded the area with an army, defeated the brigands and sacked the castle, leaving it in ruins.

The defeated baron built another castle some distance from the ruins. He was unable to replace his army, but still did not give up his evil nature. Being a stingy and greedy man, he hoarded what he had and would never give so much as a piece of bread to a starving beggar. He would as soon set the dogs on a man as help him.

The baron had an eight-year-old son, who was just as mean and cruel. 'Like father, like son!' was what the people said. One day, an old woman came to the gates begging for food. The boy happened to be playing nearby. When he saw her he yelled, "Go away, you horrid old witch, or I will set the dogs on you!"

"My dear child," said the old woman, "have pity on me. I am hungry and want just a piece of bread." The boy called the dogs and they rushed snarling at the woman. At this, she cursed him. "Unmerciful breed!" she cried. "You vile raven, sit on the ruins of your old castle and live only on the bread for which you will have to beg!"

In that instant, the boy became a raven who flew croaking and cawing to the top of the old ruins. There he sat on the remains of the tower looking at the new castle in the distance and at all his lands about him. Because of the spell, the raven could not return to his castle but had to spend his days and nights by the ruins.

One day a young boy who lived nearby came to play at the old castle. He was chewing on a piece of bread which the raven, being very

114

hungry, attempted to wrestle from him. The boy broke off a piece and gave it to the bird, who ate it greedily and begged for more. This amused the boy so much that he fed the raven all the rest of his bread. From then on, the boy came nearly every day to feed the raven and play with it.

When the young baronet disappeared, a great sorrow and a great uneasiness came upon his family and their attendants. They searched everywhere, but there was no sign of him. He had just vanished from the face of the earth. Although his father was a stingy man, he offered a princely reward for the return of his son.

In the meantime, the boy lived in the ruins of the old castle. He was always conscious of the fact that he was a human being who had been changed into a raven. He began to understand that he had sinned because of his lack of mercy and kindness to others. He understood that it was not good to act as he and his father did.

Living in the ruins was not so bad in the summer but, when winter came, the raven almost perished. His friend, the village boy, had not shown up for several days, so the half-frozen bird made his way to the home of the boy and pecked on the window. The boy quickly ran out and brought in his shivering friend.

"Oh you poor thing! It must be cold for you in those ruins," said the boy. "It will be warm for you here and I will share my food with you." He asked his father if he could keep the bird.

"Yes, Ivan," said the father. "He is harming no one and it is cold outside. It is fine with me."

The boy said to the bird, "See, father said I can keep you here. Are you hungry? Do you want some bread?" The raven nodded his head.

"Oh, my God!" exclaimed the mother. "He understands what we say! Perhaps he is a bewitched human being!"

The whole family came to love the raven. He played with the children and became very happy. So passed the time. The boy and the bird were inseparable companions, whether pasturing the cattle or working in the fields nearby.

One day, as young Ivan was reading a book which he had brought home from school, he saw that the bird was listening very attentively. "Do you understand what I am reading?" asked the boy. The raven eagerly nodded his head.

"Are you perhaps a bewitched person?" The raven nodded that it was so.

"Are you perhaps a peasant?" A shake of the head said no.

"Then you must be of the nobility. Are you as rich as our knight, the baron?" The raven nodded his head three times.

"Well, my unfortunate friend, whether you are rich or poor is all the same to me. But I must find some way to save you from your fate. If only I knew what to do!"

Discussing this revelation, the parents remembered that, some years ago, the son of the baron had mysteriously disappeared. Much as they feared to, they went to see the baron to explain what they feared had happened to his son. At first, he refused to see them but, at the mention of his lost son, they were admitted to his presence. They told him the story of the raven, but he did not believe in such nonsense and scoffed at them. The baroness, however, insisted that they should at least go and see this strange bird. The baron grudgingly agreed.

When they arrived at the home of the peasants, the raven became very excited at the sight of his parents and hopped over to the baroness, cawing and stroking her hands with his beak. To their anxious question if he was their son he eagerly nodded yes. When his parents wanted to take him home, the raven tried to make them understand that, because of the spell, he could go no further than the ruins.

Saddened, the baron and his wife went home alone. The baron now realized that this was a punishment for his cruelty and disregard for others and that his son was paying for it. From that day on, he was a changed man. He began to be kinder to his serfs, he started to pray, and he built some churches.

One day, young Ivan went to the nearby forest to pick berries. As he was filling his pail, he saw an old man sitting under a tree.

"Glory be to Jesus Christ!" he called.

"Glory be, forever!" was the reply.

The man continued, "I am glad that you came, as I need help. I am ill, hungry and thirsty. Please do not leave me, a helpless man."

"How can I leave you? Here, eat some of these berries. Then I will take you home with me where you can stay until you are well."

"May God bless you!" said the man. "You have shown me that you are good and kind and, for that, good fortune will smile upon you. I know that you wish to save the young baronet and that you do not know how. Listen and I will tell you what to do.

"Go over the mountains, through the valleys and across many rivers until you come to a very high mountain. That mountain is the home of a bewitched country. On the top of the mountain, you will find a large garden with a well in its middle. Every hour, a hand rises from the well and from its fingers flows a spray of water with magical properties. One of these properties is the power to remove a curse from a bewitched person. If you get some of that water and sprinkle it on your raven, he will return to his original form.

"There is one problem," continued the man. "An old hag with nine heads guards the well. Eight of her heads sleep while one watches, and they take turns. If you can escape the eyes of the hag, cut off the head that is awake first, then the other eight. You can then get some of the water and save your friend. Take my sword; you will have need of it! In order to find the well you will need the assistance of an old hermit who lives at the foot of the mountain. He will direct you to the accursed country and to its well. Go, and good luck to you."

Ivan thanked the old man and went home to prepare for his journey. He told his parents about the old man and his advice and said that he was willing and eager to undertake this quest. They tried to talk him out of it, but he replied that saving his friend was more important to him than all the dangers he could face.

He set out on his journey and, after many days of hard travelling, reached the mountain where the hermit lived. Here he was again warned of the many dangers that would face him, but he was determined to carry out his mission. The hermit gave him a ball of twine, telling him to throw it to the ground at the foot of the mountain. It would then unravel and lead him right to the enchanted well. He also warned the boy never to look behind him no matter what frightening noises or voices he would hear; otherwise, he would be eaten by the fearsome creatures that lived there.

"Be careful," said the hermit. "The path is narrow and goes up a very steep slope. When you reach the top, again do not look behind you or you will be turned to stone. When you reach the well, note the hag carefully and see which of her heads is not sleeping. Wait till she is looking the other way, then quickly cut off the head that is awake. The other eight will not awaken, so they will be easy to deal with.

"Wait for the hand in the well; when it appears, fill your flask with the water and sprinkle it in the four directions of the earth. Do not be alarmed at the change that will take place. A large city will appear whose people will bless you and thank you for saving them from their curse. They will name you their ruler and you will become rich and popular. But be very careful along the way and make sure the hag does not see you first, or she will turn you to stone. Now go, and God bless you."

Ivan threw the ball of twine on the path and it unwound up a steep and slippery slope. When he was well on his way, a loud crashing and yelling greeted him: "Get out of the way! There is a large rock rolling down upon you! Give me your hand before it crushes you!" There was indeed a large rock rolling down at him, but he dodged it and it went on by, and he refused to pay any heed to the yelling.

Farther on, writhing snakes covered the path, hissing and coiling around his legs. He crossed himself three times and cut his way through with his sword. Then a pack of wolves lunged at him and a voice yelled, "Come back or they will tear you to pieces!"

This was getting to be too much for Ivan, so he yelled loudly at the voices: "Out of my way, you miserable creatures!" and beat the wolves out of his way with his sword.

As he progressed, there were many other attempts to stop him, the final one being a huge dragon who roared at him and blew fire and smoke all over the forest. After a fierce and violent battle, Ivan slew the dragon. He then found that his path was much easier.

As he began to come near the top, he heard someone weeping and begging for mercy and then screaming wildly. Ivan was losing patience with all the racket so, finally, he shouted: "Enough of this! I am the boss here, so shut up!" The noises ceased and all was still.

At last the ball of twine unwound completely at the foot of the well. Watching carefully, Ivan saw the eight heads of the hag sleeping while the ninth was looking the other way. Springing quickly at her, he swung his sword and cut off her head. The other eight heads did not awaken, so the rest was simple. Breathing more easily, he fell to his knees and thanked God for his good luck.

He sat and waited and, when the hand in the well appeared, he filled his flask with the miraculous water. He poured some into his hand and sprinkled it in the four directions of the earth. Soon, a great city took shape and a large crowd of people surrounded him, singing and thanking him for releasing them from their curse. They carried him to the palace and crowned him as their tsar.

After resting some time in his tsardom, the new ruler made plans to return to the village of his parents. He was most eager to finish his task and restore his friend to his original form.

At home, he found everyone well; they, in turn, were happy to see him back safe. He sprinkled some of the magic water on the raven, who was immediately transformed into a handsome youth. The young baronet embraced his savior and thanked him for all he had done.

"My friend, do not thank me. If I have done any good, it was because it was the will of God that I should save you and the unfortunate people of the enchanted tsardom. But now, let us go and see your parents. I want to ask them to free my mother and father from serfdom so that they can accompany me to my tsardom."

The baron admitted the two youths to his presence. Still being somewhat skeptical, he asked for proof that this was truly his son. The baroness asked about a gold locket on a chain that she had given her son and about a black mole on his left shoulder. The youth had the locket around his neck and, when he bared his shoulder, they could see the mole. The baron and baroness were convinced that this was their son.

The baron was so happy to have his son returned to him that he arranged for a huge ball to celebrate the occasion. He invited all the neighboring knights and nobility and even some commoners to the affair.

At the banquet, the young baronet told his story and the story of how Ivan had made the dangerous journey to save him. He begged his parents to allow him to go to the new tsardom with Ivan, as his servant. Ivan, however, embraced him, saying that he would be happy to have him there, but only as his minister and advisor. The baron and baroness agreed, with the condition that he visit them once a year.

Installed in his tsardom with his advisor and his family, Tsar Ivan ruled wisely and justly for many, many years. With such a benevolent ruler, his people prospered and were happy.

Squire Kotsky

Once a man had a Cat that was so old it was not able to catch mice any more. The man got tired of feeding the Cat and getting nothing in return, so he abandoned it out in the forest, just to be rid of it.

A Fox came along and saw the Cat sitting under a tree. "Who are you?" she asked.

"I am Squire Kotsky."

"Would you like to marry me and be my husband?" asked the Fox.

"So be it," was his reply.

They went to her house and had dinner. How she tried to please him! When she caught a hen, she would not eat any of it until she had taken it home for him to share.

One day, a Hare said to the Fox, "Good day to you, Sister Fox. Some day soon I must come to visit you at your home."

The Fox replied, "Squire Kotsky now lives at my house, and he would tear you to pieces."

The frightened Hare told the Wolf about Squire Kotsky, the Wolf told the Wild Boar, and the Boar told the Bear. All four met in order to plan how they should meet this Squire Kotsky.

"Let us prepare a dinner," they said, "and let each of us bring some food."

The Wolf said, "I will bring some meat and bones for borsch."

The Boar said, "I will bring a bunch of beets and some potatoes."

The Bear said, "I will bring a big pot of honey for dessert."

The Hare said, "I will bring some cabbage and some carrots."

Then they had to decide who would go and invite Squire Kotsky to dinner. This could be a very dangerous thing to do!

The Bear said, "I would not be able to run away if he got angry at me."

The Boar said, "I also am not very nimble."

The Wolf said, "I am old and do not see too well. I would be in danger if he got angry at me."

The Hare said, "I guess I am chosen to go and invite Squire Kotsky to dinner."

The Hare ran to where the Fox and Squire Kotsky lived and called out, "Sister Fox, please come out and speak with me."

When the Fox saw the Hare standing there, quivering and ready to flee, she asked, "What have you come here for?"

"The Bear, the Boar, the Wolf and I are inviting you and Squire Kotsky for dinner."

"Thank you, we will come. But you had better hide, for he will tear you to pieces."

The Hare scampered back to the others and reported. "Sister Fox said he would come, but we should all hide, or he will tear us to pieces."

The Boar said, "I will hide by the table in this pile of brush."

The Wolf said, "I will hide myself here behind this bush."

The Bear said, "I will hide up in this tree."

The Hare said, "I will hide myself deep in this bramble-bush."

The Fox came, leading Squire Kotsky. When they got to the table and the Cat saw all the food, he cried, "Miaow! Miaow!"

The hidden animals thought he was yelling "More! More!" and feared that if the food was not enough, Squire Kotsky would eat them too.

Squire Kotsky jumped up onto the table and began to gobble the food noisily. Having had his fill, he stretched out on the table to rest.

The Boar, hiding in the pile of brush by the table, was afraid to breathe, but soon a mosquito began to bite his tail. He began switching his tail to get rid of the mosquito.

The Cat, thinking the switching was a mouse, grabbed the Boar by the tail. The frightened Boar jumped up and ran away as fast as he could, knocking over the table in his haste. Squire Kotsky, startled by the commotion, leaped straight up into the tree.

The Bear thought Squire Kotsky was coming after him, so he climbed higher and higher up the tree. The tree was too skinny, and it bent under the weight of the Bear. Finally, the Bear lost his grip and fell with a thump right on top of the Wolf.

They both jumped up and sped off as fast as their legs would carry them. The Hare, of course, had long since disappeared.

Much later, the four frightened animals met, a long way from home. "Such a small animal," they said, "but he almost ate us all up!"

Timmy Telesyk

Once, long ago and far away, an old couple lived near a river. They were very old, and were getting older every day. As they had no children, they began to worry about their future. "Who will look after us when we get too old to do things for ourselves?" they said.

The old woman said to the old man: "Go into the forest and get some nice wood to make a little cradle. If I put a little wooden doll into it and rock it, I can pretend that we have a child and my life will be easier."

At first, the old man was not sure about this but, finally, he went to the forest and cut down a small poplar tree. He took the tree home and made a cradle and a rough wooden doll.

The old woman put the doll in the cradle and, as she rocked, she sang a song:

"Oh Telesyk, boy so sweet,
With hands so small and tiny feet.
I will cook for you some wheat;
So come and sit with me and eat."

She rocked the cradle all day long and went to bed happy. In the morning, she found that her doll had become a live little boy cooing and squirming in the cradle. The old couple were so happy that they wept. They loved their little boy, and named him Timmy Telesyk. They named him 'Timmy' because that was the name of the old man and 'Telesyk' because that means 'one who squirms.'

When he got older, Timmy Telesyk said to his father: "Father, make me a boat of gold with silver oars. I will go fishing and help to feed us."

Father made a little boat painted gold and oars painted silver, and put the boat in the river. Every day after that, Timmy Telesyk went fishing and provided food for his family.

He would go out in the morning, catch some fish, take them to his mother and go out fishing again. His mother took his breakfast to him on the riverbank and told him: "If I call to you, come to the shore but, if a stranger calls to you, row away to the middle of the river."

When Timmy Telesyk heard his mother calling out to him:

"Timmy Telesyk, come to shore.
Here is food and drink and more,"

he would say to his boat:

"Float, float, my little boat,
Take me to the shore.
It is time to eat;
My mother calls me over."

One day, a Dragon heard Mother calling Timmy Telesyk to the riverbank. The Dragon hid herself in the bushes and tried calling him in her deep, deep Dragon voice:

"Timmy Telesyk, come to shore.
Here is food and drink and more."

When Timmy Telesyk heard the deep voice, he knew it was not his mother. He said:

"Float, float, my little boat,
Take me now much farther out."

He swung his oar strongly and the boat floated away from the shore.

The Dragon waited and waited for Timmy Telesyk to come to the shore and, when he did not, she went away sulking.

At noon Mother prepared a lunch, went to the riverbank and called out:

"Timmy Telesyk, come to shore.
Here is food and drink and more."

Timmy Telesyk said to his boat:

"Float, float, my little boat,
Take me to the shore.
It is time to eat;
My mother calls me over."

He went to the shore, gave his mother his catch, ate his lunch and pushed the boat out into the river again. When Mother had gone, the Dragon again tried to call Timmy Telesyk in her deep, deep Dragon voice:

"Timmy Telesyk, come to shore.
Here is food and drink and more."

Timmy Telesyk knew it was not his mother calling. He said:

"Float, float, my little boat,
Take me now much farther out."

The boat floated away from shore and the Dragon again went away angry.

Seeing that she was not getting any results this way, the Dragon went to the blacksmith and said to him, "Blacksmith, make me a voice that sounds like the mother of Timmy Telesyk." The blacksmith dared not refuse, and he made the voice for the Dragon.

The Dragon went back to the riverbank and called with her new voice:

"Timmy Telesyk, come to shore.
Here is food and drink and more."

Timmy Telesyk thought, "That is my mother with my supper." He said:

"Float, float, my little boat,
Take me to the shore.
It is time to eat;
My mother calls me over."

When the boat reached shore, the Dragon jumped out of the bushes, grabbed Timmy Telesyk from the boat and carried him away. Coming to her house, she called out: "Little Dragon Olenka, open up the door." Little Dragon Olenka opened the door and the Dragon took Timmy Telesyk inside.

"Little Dragon Olenka, build a big fire in the pich. Make it hot enough to split rocks, and bake this Telesyk while I go and invite some guests to our feast," said the Dragon, and away she went.

Little Dragon Olenka heated the pich and put in some rocks. When it was so hot that the rocks split she said, "Timmy Telesyk, sit on this shovel so I can put you in the pich."

133

"But I do not know how to sit on a shovel," said Timmy Telesyk.

"Never mind about how, just sit on it," said Little Dragon Olenka.

He put one of his hands on the shovel. "Like this?" he asked.

"No, no! Sit on it, sit on it!"

He put his head on the shovel. "Like this?"

"No, no, no! Sit on it!"

"I do not know how," said Timmy Telesyk. "Could you please show me?"

Little Dragon Olenka was very angry; she sat right on the shovel, put her hands on her hips and said, "Like this, you stupid boy!"

Timmy Telesyk, quick as a wink, grabbed the shovel, thrust Little Dragon Olenka into the pich and shut the door. He locked up the house, climbed into a tall maple tree and waited.

After a while the Dragon came back with her guests. "Little Dragon Olenka, open up the door," she called. There was no answer and, of course, the door did not open. She called again, "Little Dragon Olenka, open up the door," and still there was no reply.

Thinking that Little Dragon Olenka had gone away somewhere, the Dragon opened the door herself. She and her friends all went in and sat around the table. The Dragon opened the pich, pulled out what she thought was baked Telesyk and served the guests.

After they had finished eating, they all tumbled outside and rolled on the grass, singing:

"I will tumble and roll,
After eating Telesyk whole!"

Timmy Telesyk sang from his tree:

"Yes, tumble and roll,
But you have eaten Olenka whole!"

The Dragons stopped, but they did not quite hear what Timmy Telesyk said, so they carried on rolling on the grass and singing :

"I will tumble and roll,
After eating Telesyk whole!"

Again Timmy Telesyk sang out:

"Yes, tumble and roll,
But you have eaten Olenka whole!"

The Dragons stopped and listened. This time they heard it clearly, but they did not know what it meant. They searched around to find where the voice was coming from and one of them spotted Timmy Telesyk in the maple tree.

All the Dragons gathered around the tree and began to gnaw on its trunk. They chewed and chewed, but the tree was too hard and they broke their teeth. They went to the blacksmith and said, "Blacksmith, make us some teeth that are strong enough to gnaw down a maple tree."

The blacksmith forged them new teeth and they returned to gnaw on the tree. Now they could chew great big pieces out of its trunk.

A flock of geese was flying overhead and Timmy Telesyk called to them:

"Geese and goslings, in the sky;
Take me home, and help me fly.
I will feed you with my hand
And keep you safe upon my land."

The geese replied: "We cannot stop. Let the next flock pick you up." The Dragons were resting their weary jaws but, soon, began to gnaw again. Then, the tree began to creak.

Another flock of geese flew over and Timmy Telesyk called to them:

"Geese and goslings, in the sky;
Take me home, and help me fly.
I will feed you with my hand
And keep you safe upon my land."

The geese replied: "We cannot stop. Let the next geese pick you up." By this time, the tree was beginning to lean and Timmy Telesyk was getting very worried. Finally, one lone gosling came struggling along, hardly able to fly. Timmy Telesyk called out desperately;

"Little gosling in the sky;
Take me home, and help me fly.
I will feed you with my hand
And keep you safe upon my land."

The gosling flew down and put Timmy Telesyk on her back. With the extra weight, she could barely stay in the air and she flew as best she could just above the ground. The Dragons all chased the pair, but were unable to catch them.

The gosling took Timmy Telesyk home, left him on a windowsill and rested on the grass. Inside, Timmy Telesyk could see his father at the table and his mother at the pich. Mother took some fresh tarts out of the pich and said, "Here is one for Father and one for Mother."

Outside, Timmy Telesyk said loudly, "And how about one for me?"

Mother thought she heard something, but she did not know what it was. She took more tarts from the pich and said again, "Here is one for Father and one for Mother."

Timmy Telesyk again loudly called out, "How about one for me?"

Mother heard something this time. "Do you hear that?" she said to her husband. "I think someone is calling."

"I heard nothing," he replied. "Maybe it is the wind that you hear."

Mother took more tarts from the pich and again said, but more loudly this time, "Here is one for Father and one for Mother."

"How about me?" hollered Timmy Telesyk.

"I did hear someone calling," said Mother. She looked out the window and saw Timmy Telesyk sitting on the windowsill. Mother and Father ran outside and carried Timmy Telesyk into the house. They were so happy to see him!

Mother had seen the gosling on the grass. "I will cook that gosling," she said. "We can have a nice feast to celebrate."

Timmy Telesyk said, "No, Mother. Give the gosling some millet and let it be. If it were not for the gosling, I would not be here today."

They fed the gosling, gave it some millet for its trip, and off it flew. Timmy Telesyk told his mother and father the whole story, and Mother took some more tarts out of the pich. She said, "Here is one for Father and one for Mother, and here is one for Timmy Telesyk."

Notes on the Tales

Page 11 The Bear From That Other World

From my grandfather's tattered old book, this tale is similar to several other stories from Eastern Europe. For example, similarities may be seen between this story and the many versions of the Russian Firebird tales.

Page 25 The Clever Daughter

This story has been told and retold in many, many books. In its varied forms, it is to be found in collections from numerous countries.

Page 33 The Cossack and the Spider

An example of how stories cross borders and adapt to cultures which likely did not originate them. This is a very well-known Scottish tale which was told to me in Ukrainian by my mother when I was quite young. She does not remember where she heard the story but, with its characters and setting, it appears to have entered the body of Ukrainian folklore.

Page 35 The Cranberry Tree

Found in numerous collections, with varying details. Often, for example, the sopilka is made from a reed growing in a lake where a child was drowned. This version was told to me by my father, who does not remember where or when he first ran across it.

Page 41   The Deceitful Nanny Goat

One of many folk tales with repeated rhyming elements. The Nanny Goat's warning to the animals, for example, is repeated many times in exactly the same words.

Page 49   The Enchanted Castle

A unique story, in that I have found it only once, in my grandfather's old book. Certain elements are similar to those of other stories but, in its entirety, this story has no twins.

Page 57   The Flying Ship

One of the most oft-told tales from Ukraine. Often it is said to be Russian but, as is the case with so many things Ukrainian, it is simply a case of ignorance on the part of the story collectors. Due in large part to Russian efforts to eradicate Ukrainian culture and tradition, misinformation about Ukraine abounds. The realm of folklore is not immune to this pervasive and deliberate Russian propaganda.

Page 73   The Frog Princess

This story appears in many clothes from many lands. Similar to The Frog Prince and such tales from other countries, it does, nevertheless, follow its own narrative line.

Page 89   The Gossip

Another common Ukrainian folk tale often attributed to Russia. This version was compiled from no fewer than ten different renditions of the story found in various collections.

Page 95   The Little Golden Harp

Remembered by my father, who heard it when he was very young from "some men" who came to the farm in Saskatchewan one Christmas in the early 1900s. It is often told at Christmastime in the Podilia region of Ukraine.

Page 100   The Poplar and the Greedy Woman

This tale also appears with varying details. The magic is sometimes made by a red or golden fish, but the story line is the same. In Ukraine the tree is usually a linden tree but, since in Canada the linden is not as well-known as the poplar, it may be that the change is nothing less than a Canadianization of the tale.

Page 105   The Raspberry Hut

Another story from my grandfather's old book. I have not found any tales at all similar to this one in any of the hundreds of collections I have studied. I liked the idea of a Raspberry Hut, hence the title for this book.

Page 113   The Raven

Another unique tale from my grandfather's old book. Again, I have found no tales anywhere which are quite like this one, although the magic is similar to that in many other stories.

Page 125   Squire Kotsky

A fairly popular Ukrainian story. Quite often, the cat is called Sir or Pan Kotsky, but the story is essentially the same.

Page 129   Timmy Telesyk

This story is another common one, which is found in several collections. The young lad is often called Ivanko or Ivan, and details vary considerably, but the story is the same.

— Danny Evanishen, Editor

In this glossary:

[a] is pronounced as in f<u>a</u>r
[e] is pronounced as in g<u>e</u>t
[ee] is pronounced as in f<u>ee</u>t
[i] is pronounced as in s<u>i</u>t
[o] is pronounced as between g<u>o</u>t and g<u>oa</u>t
[oo] is pronounced as in l<u>oo</u>se
[y] is pronounced as in <u>y</u>es

[zh] is pronounced as in vi<u>si</u>on